Social Media for Real Businesses

How to balance on-line and face to face sales and marketing for best results.

Dr Alan Rae – Chairman
Free Spirits Ltd

Author: © Dr Alan Rae 2011

The right of Alan Rae to be identified as the author of this work has been asserted in accordance with the Copyright, Designs and Patents Act 1988

Alan can be contacted on 0845 094 0407 or at alan@howtodobusiness.com

Publishing History 1st Edition 2011

Title: Social Media for real Businesses

Published by:

Free Spirits Ltd
The Glasshouses
Fletching Common
Newick, Lewes, BN8 4JJ

ISBN number 9 781849 141383

Table of Contents

Call to action

This book is aimed at helping you as a business owner get the most out of your sales marketing and networking and will help you decide when and where to use social media.

It's based on interviews with lots of businesses like yours – some that are bumping along the bottom and others who are real pioneers in the art of making a little money go a long way and turn their marketing activity into real leads that come with less effort than doing it long-hand.

This is real marketing – based on what real people do backed up with our own experiences of running several businesses – usually employing around 10 or so – since 1981.

Since 2005 nearly 2000 companies have completed one of our questionnaires and we've held over 60 in-depth interviews with early adopters who have good stories to tell.

Some have really innovative projects for collaborative working or social networking sites. Others apply web 2.0 principles to quite ordinary businesses such as Independent Financial Advisors, Solicitors or Technical Authoring businesses.

This book distils their experiences into an approach that you practically use.

Marketing for a small business is largely about Lead Generation. You choose a product or service that appeals to a large enough customer base and construct a story and look and feel to appeal emotionally to the customers you want to attract.

Then you have to tell it face to face, in writing and on line as many times as it takes to get the business you need.

You need a shrewd idea of what your business model actually is – and how much activity you need to make it happen. Then monitor it to keep it on track.

And above all you need to be clear how much of your activity should be face to face and how much should be using the new media of the internet. That's what this book is obout.

The book at a glance

I want to help you get the most from promoting your business so this book is divided in two parts – Theory and Practice.

In the theory section we're going to cover issues like how networks operate and how you can analyse and extend the networks you already belong to achieve more leverage in the market place.

We'll look at the dynamics of markets and how psychological forces drive them and we consider how you can develop a story that connects your ways of looking at the world, your needs and values with those of your customers.

We consider how many times you need to tell your story and where this should occur. We outline the principles of building a sales pyramid and help you think through how many enquiries you need to get the sales you require.

This depends on what sort of business you have. I'll help you answer the critical question of how much time should you be spending on line and how much you should use face to face selling and networking.

We'll review the tools that you have available to you and we'll discuss these in the light of what other companies like yourself have done. We carried out a research project in which nearly 800 small businesses in Europe, Asia and the US told us what marketing techniques they used. I've distilled what we found out to help you market yourself better.

This combines with our own experiences of running several businesses in our own company. These include online sales of plants and gardening equipment as well as my Market Research and Business consultancy.

In the practical section of the book, we'll look at the online tools available to you.

We'll review the various social networking sites like Facebook, Ecademy and Linked-in and cover how you can use tools like Twitter, YouTube and Slideshare to develop your position as an expert in your field so that you have a top-class set of scenery to back up the face to face activity that is the bedrock of how you get enquiries and referrals.

I'll show you how to identify the relevant keywords that are used to tag items and drive traffic, how to write things once and have them appear in the information streams your customers use and how to work with the way people think, behave, gain information and recommend and advocate the people they value.

Part One - Theory

Now we are always hearing about how social media and internet marketing are becoming fundamental to marketing even in the small business environment.

Books, articles, advice and courses on how to use the Tools of Web 2.0 such as

> Twitter
>
> Facebook and Linked-in
>
> Blogs
>
> You-tube
>
> Adwords
>
> Search Engine optimisation

are everywhere.

It's claimed that this is a whole new way of promoting yourself. Is this just Hype? Or reality?

How much time and money should you spend on this vs. conventional sales and marketing? And what about networking – that other 21st Century panacea for changing the performance of your business?

The key question we have to ask ourselves is

WHAT IS THE RIGHT BALANCE FOR MY SPECIFIC BUSINESS?

Not someone else's

As always it depends on who you are and what you're doing.

For a service business, where you have to deliver as well as promote yourself, chances are you need all the help you can get. Anything that can get your story out to the right people, inexpensively and get them to come to you has got to be a benefit – because really you don't have the time any more to prospect for customers in the way we did in the '80s.

But there's a real change in the way people react to marketing. Intrusion marketing is dead. Spam and intrusive telephone calls just irritate potential customers. We've all trained ourselves to ignore or fast forward through advertising. Hence the rise of permission marketing – where people subscribe to hear what you say. Sign-ups for newsletters, blogs, membership of social media sites and twitter – which is pure permission marketing – all have their role to play.

This move to permission marketing is a reaction to the transactional style of the '80s and '90s. There are plenty of people who believe in purposeful, targeted marketing (about half according to our survey) but a growing percentage sees value in random activity., As practical business people we have to ask under what circumstances does it make sense to spend time looking for random connections.?

Thomas Power, chairman of Ecademy, which was one of the pioneering on-line social networks, believes that you have to find the 50 people in the world who are most important to your business.

Who these people are and how you find them is central to our discussion.

If you run a local, non-scalable business – like our Fletching Glasshouses organic veg concern, then all of these important 50 people are likely to be found by face to face networking, referrals and a bit of turning up in person.

If it's a national, scalable business like our www.plants4presents.co,uk business or an international consultancy business like www.howtodobusiness.com then the value of making random connections is greater and your 50 people will be much more widely dispersed.

We all have to decide what mixture of purposeful and random, local and national, face to face and on-line activity we need to make. How you achieve this is what this book is about.

Business is both and art and a science. And it's about relationships AND transactions.

Business as it is taught on MBA courses and practiced in the corporate world is all about transactions. And control. And becoming the Gorilla that dominates the niche it occupies.

Business as it is described by the apostles of social media claim its all about relationships, holding conversations with your customers and making random connections. It's about having a tango with the market place- setting out your stall and following the money.

Now it's true that without a good relationship with your customers you haven't got a business in the long term and it's equally true that if you haven't got any transactions (or any systematic way of delivering the value you promise) then you haven't got one in the short term either.

So the art is to blend these two principles, control and transactions on the one hand with vision and relationships on the other.   This represents a synthesis of left and right brain thinking which is why we go into the psychology of markets and developing stories in a bit of depth.

Thomas and Penny Power who run the Ecademy social business site describe the mindsets as Open Random and Supportive vs. Closed, Selective and Controlling.

If you are selling to the local community then talking to the people you know will buy your stuff may be a logical strategy.

If you want to play on a larger stage, chances are you will need more random connections to get the numbers you need. In fact our research has demonstrated that people who have a national or international focus are twice as likely to use online methods for connection.

You have to choose the balance you have to strike.

A good policy is to decide how much randomness you need and then inject it into your business model by spending an equivalent amount of time in "high randomness" environments like Twitter or Ecademy. If you want to be "purposeful" because you're operating in a local or in a small closed industry like Aerospace, then close networking groups or Linked In will give better results.

Most of us need a bit of each – sorting out the mix is what this book is about.

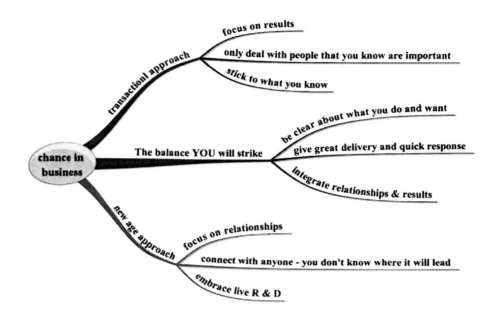

This diagram illustrates the characteristics of these general strategies.

The three prongs on the Balance line in the diagram tell us something interesting. Whatever strategy you take – whether predominantly online or face to face – you will find the same rules of behaviour apply.

Research reveals three things necessary for successful networking

be clear about what you do,

Get back to people quickly

Develop a reputation as a good collaborator.

Small Business Marketing

Running a business is about getting enough work and delivering it on time – and profitably. Most small businesses these days are in the service sector – business or personal. If the owner is delivering the service then this limits the amount of time that can be spent on promotion.

Our research tells us that the average business person spends 12-15 hours a week on promotion. That's everything – face to face sales, networking, online activity, and conventional offline marketing.

Business comes in various ways

>   You can go looking for it
>
>   You can advertise for it
>
>   You can encourage other people to recommend you by networking
>
>   You can create a marketing presence which will drive traffic to your site or to you via the phone.

However, we all know that when you're selling you're not working and when you're working you're not selling. In order to square this circle, you have to work smarter. You need to encourage people to come to you – so you need to be generating a flow of warm leads.

For this to happen, you need a compelling story that links you to the customer and you need to tell it often enough, and in the right places

Face to Face

On-line

In writing.

to generate the sales enquiries that you need.

Professional marketers call this the marketing mix

I can't tell you how many enquiries you need – that depends on your business model and how good you are at selling.

But I can tell you how to work it out – and if you insist – I can hold you accountable to your figures. Because after all – you're not reading this for the good of your health – you want to get some results.

Don't you?

What's your story?

You need a narrative that connects you to the customer and motivates them to work with you. It's really important to get this right as you can also use it inside the organisation to motivate your staff. If we tell this story outside the business it's called marketing. If we tell it inside the business it's called leadership – but it's the same story.

It needs to be

Compelling
Engaging emotionally to the listener
Phrased in their language
Addressed to their pain so it will spur them into action

It has to be absolutely crystal clear and unambiguous about what you do and why.

All our research shows that people give business or refer business to people that they're clear about what they do. So you have to really work hard to hone this down. We're all tempted to believe we can get more business by occupying more of the canvas to attract more people. Don't do it. Focus – be the best you can be at what you do and make sure people know that. And if you can – be unique! It's a fundamental principle of marketing that whatever you do you should dominate something – doesn't matter how small it is – just dominate it.

Current research suggests that people buy things that are

Simple

Relevant

Authentic

The benefit of being number 1 in a niche is shown here. We get caught out by the idea that change is continuous – it isn't.

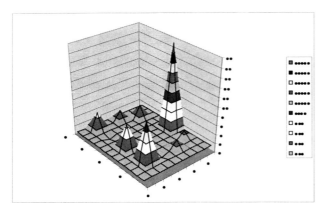

A power law describes what happens in markets – and in networks.

The most connected or market leader will typically have twice the market share of the next player, three times the third player and so on.

On the face of it being 3rd or 4th doesn't sound too bad. But let's look at it as a picture. You can see that the number one has an over whelming advantage.

Once the market has reached this stage its all over for everyone else. In today's cyber world this can happen surprisingly quickly

Scary isn't it

Geoffrey Moore says that in each mature market there is a Gorilla, 2 or 3 chimps and lots of monkeys. [i] Much strategic marketing is about identifying niches in which you can be the Gorilla!

To achieve the dominance you want you need to be clear about what you're doing for whom – and how it helps them.

We are all trained to think we should talk about benefits but that's not the best way forward. People are mainly motivated by fear, greed and fashion – although when acting as individuals, freedom, indulgence and altruism also have roles.

The research suggests that the drive for freedom is what prompts people to set up businesses in the first place. But here's a secret.

IN BUSINESS DECISION MAKERS ARE MOSTLY MOTIVATED BY FEAR.

Fear of failure – Fear of losing what they've so carefully built. Fear of losing control. Visionaries are motivated by possibilities and some are motivated by making money. But many, many more are motivated by fear.

If they have a problem – and you can show them a safe, affordable solution you have a stronger chance of making the sale than playing on their desire for expansion.

So you have to know what worries them.

> Not enough sales,
> Can't generate leads
> Cash flow
> Getting their project – whatever it is completed.

And then show them how whatever you do will get them off the hook – in a way that leaves them in control of their organisation.

But – you have to know that you're talking to them in the right language. Because if you're story doesn't resonate with them – you're going nowhere.

So it's worth spending a bit of time to understand a bit more how people are motivated – how they think – and what language a given segment of the market is like to respond to.

We talked a little bit earlier about the balance between results and transactions and between relationships and possibilities.

You won't be surprised then to hear that people who are focused on results need to be talked to differently than those who are primarily motivated by building a set of relationships or to constructing a vision of where they would like to take their business – or indeed the world.

Psychological Interlude

We all have a major blind spot – in that we see the world in a certain way that's conditioned by our own preferred thinking style, our values and what's happened to us in our lives. When we're not paying attention we often lapse back into thinking that other people see things more or less the same way as we do – but the truth is that they probably don't.

To get past this we need a framework which can help us understand

> that other people may be different
> what the main thinking styles and value systems might be
> How they see each other – what language relates well to them and how they like to be approached.

We went looking for something which was rich enough to be useful but simple enough that practical people could apply it in their day to day work – and be able to use it without going through a lengthy and expensive accreditation process.

We found this in the Brain Technologies Corporation's suite of products particularly the BrainMap® which deals with thinking styles and the MindMaker6® which deals with value systems. Most of these ideas can be found in Dudley Lynch's Seminal Book "Strategy of the Dolphin"[ii]

You are probably familiar with the idea that different people think in different ways. There is a right side to the brain which deals in patterns and a left side which deals in numbers and logic. There is a front portion of the brain which likes to think and an instinctive, old brain at the rear which operates on immediate perception and impulse. If you map these into quadrants, you get 4 styles of thinking and behaviour which have different characteristics. And we see different patterns being dominant at different stages of the business cycle.

The diagram shows, top right thinkers as "visionaries" who like to explore new things top left thinkers can be labelled as "accountants" who like control, bottom left are "entrepreneurs" who are impatient to achieve their goals and bottom right are "team players" who focus on

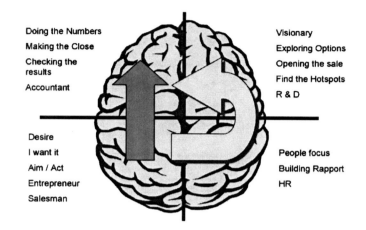

people issues. We can easily measure where we are and gain and understanding of how others tick using the Brain Technologies BrainMap.

The MindMaker6 tool uses the Graves Spiral to identify 6 major world views that people adopt. These are either group/relationships orientated or individual/results orientated. Individuals (and societies) move between systems as they become aware of the limitations of their currently most dominant mind-set. As an individual moves up the spiral, the degree of complexity in their behaviour grows. Most of us have more than one view that we can adopt but one of these will be dominant.

We believe that understanding these views and their dynamics is important to telling our story. We need to be clear about what our views and values are and those of our customers since if you talk in language that the customer feels comfortable with, you are more likely to motivate them than if you don't.

Why do we think it so important to have a working knowledge of these issues? Because you have to have in mind who you are trying to sell to and what their values are if you want to write persuasive copy.

We can map different types of organisation to represent the positions of the Graves Spiral onto the BrainMap. It looks like this.

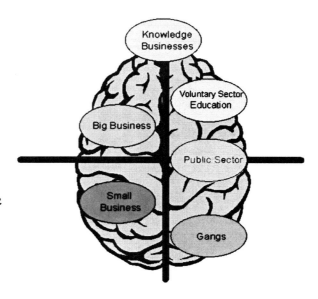

What this means is that the organisations on the left are results and self orientated while those on the right are group / relationship orientated. The individuals and organisations have a characteristic balance between instinctive and thinking behaviour.

Knowledge businesses strike a balance between technology and people issues and represent a new tendency that can make a conscious use of the other views. This is the position from which the progressive use of new media originates – it values potential random connections and is not held back by the command and control mind-set that you find in both corporate and public sector organisations.

Once you understand how these dynamics operate and the value systems they represent, you can start to express your ideas in ways that will relate better to you potential customers and get better results.

The value systems on the left are self orientated while those on the right are group orientated. Inside an organisation, if you use "me" language with "we" people they will tend to work to hold you back or keep you in your place. If you use "we" language with "me" people, they will tend to see you as weak and try to marginalise you.

System	Language	Morality
Kinsperson	Basic Earthy Alive Here – I'll show you	What will be will be
Loner	Power / Action the man I'm looking for	It's a hard cruel world
Loyalist	Crisp formal conservative We want stability	There is duty and orders – always
Achiever	Fast business / military 2nd place is 1st loser	There will always be losers
Involver	Loose ambiguous stories Address human features	We have to try
Choice-seeker	Systems language & ideas Strong learning opportunities	The rules are ambiguous

So it goes in selling or writing marketing copy. The values and appropriate language that you might use is set out here.

The concept of shared values is really important in building your narrative. Let's see if we can drill down into who you are and how you think.

These ideas are explored in more detail in our online copywriting course which makes use of both the BrainMap and the MindMaker6 tools.

But for now, see if you can map yourself on these continuums.

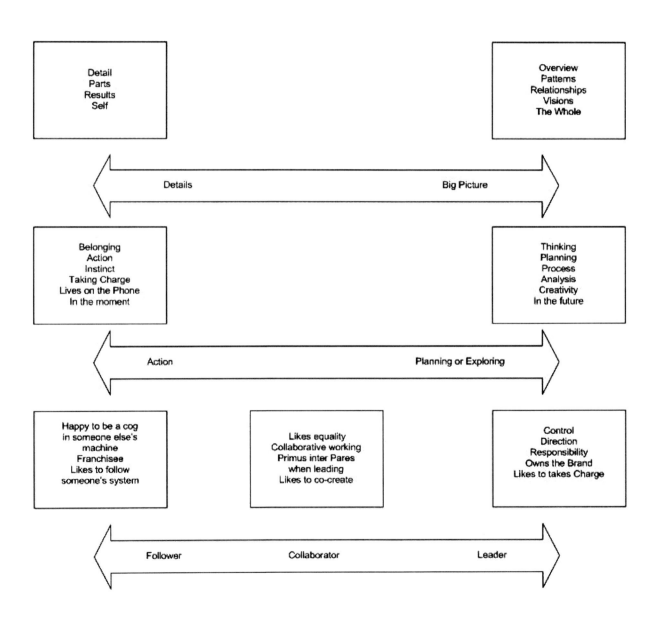

Once you've done that try to write a description of the persona of your typical or ideal customer in the same sort of terms – what's their thinking style and values look like. We'll return to this in the Practical Part 2

You might want to take into account HOW you relate to the customer. Are you focused on an innovative product – like HP and Apple, on operational excellence in delivery like Tesco or McDonalds – or on really knowing your customer like a traditional Saville Row tailor. Or a combination of two of these.

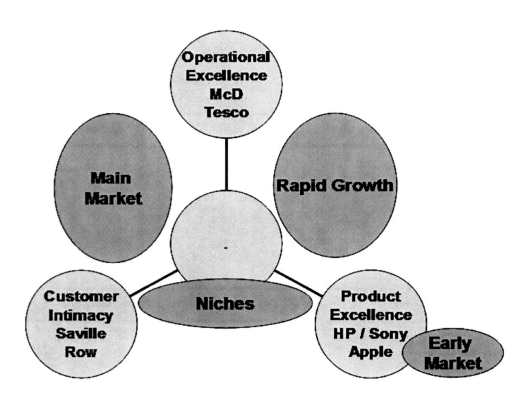

These poles relate to different positions in the product life cycle - where distinct mindsets are found.

The early market is characterised by visionaries and innovators

'It focuses on product excellence. The rapid growth phase depends on customers who value a combination of product and operational excellence while the Main Market is populated by those who value a blend of operational excellence and customer knowledge.

In the same way, appealing to niches within the main market often involves a combination of segmentation skills and unique, excellent products.

Try Describing the Persona of your ideal customer here.

Your business strategy will depend on which section of the market you and your customers occupy. On it depends how you deliver – and how you talk about what you do.

This brings us to the idea of the chasm – and is a concrete example of how important thinking styles and mindsets are – and why it's so important to understand your own – because – as any salesman will tell you – we sell most easily to those who are like us.

The Chasm is discussed in detail in 2 books by Geoffrey Moore – "Crossing the Chasm" and "Inside the Tornado". Read the second one – he summarised "Crossing the Chasm" in the first few chapters and goes on to talk about the dynamics of emerging markets and the way in which de facto standards happen. I think it's a must read for the serious marketer.

The Chasm (which is the gap that companies with innovative products often struggle with between the innovators and early adopters and the main market) is caused by the difference in mentality between visionaries and the early majority and late early adopters in the main market.

Once you've run out of people who are interested in innovation you need to speak a different language to the analytic types – accountants, project managers, who are the decision makers in the early majority. Moore was talking about high technology markets and what he describes as "pragmatists" are the IT directors who control that part of the market.

They need to be seen to be right. They don't like being exposed. They put a lot of energy into making the correct, safe choice – because that's what their career will depend on.

So they don't like change – their attitude is

Let's put it off

If we have to change we'll adopt what seems to be winning

We'll all do it at the same time

We'll get it over with as fast as possible

Hard to convince if you're a visionary – but if you do you'll hit the jackpot – because this kind of analytic herd instinct will trigger a tornado – Moore's word for the emergence of a de facto standard – like Windows, the IBM PC architecture, VHS, iPODs etc.

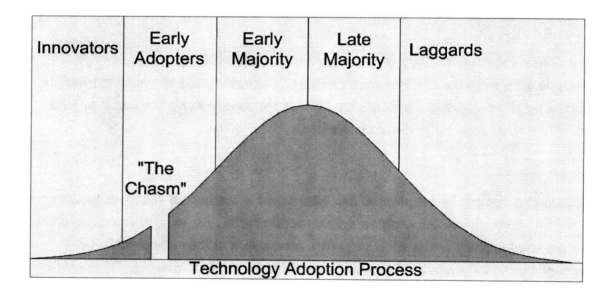

I think this underscores why understanding psychology and language is so important in marketing. So having taken all this on board – let's have a go at the Story. **Try writing out what your story is in outline here so that it appeals to the person you are talking to.**

How many leads do you need?

This is an area that many small businesses struggle with.

Obtaining orders is a numbers game. You need a clear business model that delivers so many orders per week with a sufficient gross margin to pay for costs of sale, overheads and leaving something over for re-investment and profit.

This means so many sales per week. To win those sales, a face to face business typically needs about 3 times as many live close-able prospects to achieve the sales for the profit target. This number needs to be topped up week by week. To achieve that we may need to qualify 6 times that number of leads and the marketing activity will need to generate this volume.

So whether you rely on advertising, telesales or internet based technologies, it's important to have a clear idea of what your model requires and how much it's going to take to build the sausage machine. The pattern is shown in the diagram.

It's important to measure what the conversion ratios are at each stage of the pyramid. The numbers will differ with each business but it's crucial to know what these are. That way you can monitor your own sales performance and that of anyone you later employ and need to manage.

If you do that then you can establish where things go wrong. If you know what the characteristic ratios between levels in the pyramid you can identify where you – or someone who works for you is failing. Here's an example from a face to face business like the computer dealership I used to run.

	Normal	Lazy	Can't Qualify	Can't Close
New Enquiries / Week	30	15	30	30
Suspects :Prospects	6:1	6:1	3:1	6:1
Prospects :Closes	4:1	4:1	12:1	4:1
Closes/ Negotiations : Sale	3:1	3:1	3:1	12:1
Sales per month	4	2	1	1

●

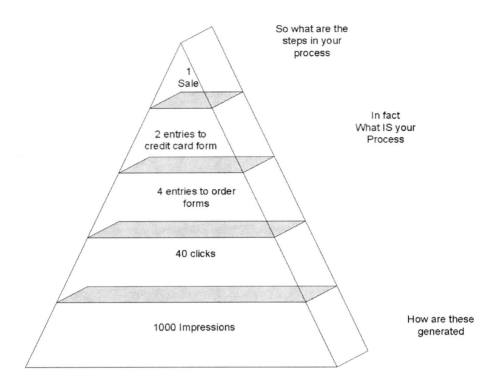

The same pattern of course exists in the on line world. If we analyse the processes we go through in our www.plants4presents.co.uk business we need to obtain impressions via paid or organic search, a certain percentage click through to the landing page. A smaller proportion goes through to the order form and so on.•

It's worth taking the time to answer the questions posed here – what is your process – what are the steps and how are they generated.

Sales experts like Grant Leboff [iii]argue that in today's world customers can't be treated mechanically so we should focus on building relationships. Nevertheless a similar amount of activity needs to take place. You still need to engage with many more people than will actually buy whether we are chasing them or they are choosing us – the numbers probably don't vary.

If you run an internet business it's critical to know the ratios of impressions to clickthroughs, and clicks to sale. If we know what the pattern should be then we can measure it. We want a low effort, least cost means to deliver the enquiries we need via a self qualification system that reduces prospecting time so we can focus on good prospects and customers.

Google Analytics is probably the tool of choice for most of us as it allows us to see what the conversion ratios are by setting goals. And Google ad words allow us to check the conversion rates on our adverts.

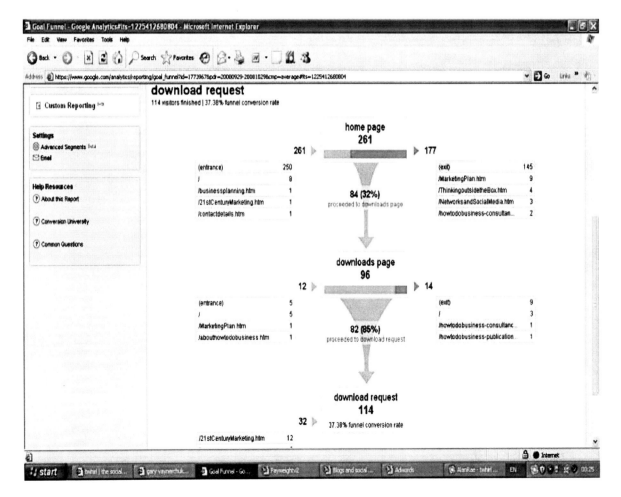

Your marketing Activity

Once the story is defined it has to be told. As you can see from the discussion we've just had, this has to be often enough and in the right places to deliver the conversion ratios you need.

Our research shows that most people spend 12-15 hours a week promoting themselves. That's everything. Networking, one to one selling, off-line marketing, online activity.

You need to be clear where your business is coming from. How much business will come from selling more stuff to existing customers, new stuff to existing customers or finding new customers for your existing products? While it's much easier to sell new products to old customers, the sad fact is that 3 times as many businesses take the hard route of looking for new outlets for their existing products. Also bear in mind that most companies lose half their customer base in 5 years (Harvard Business Review) – and that the average British company just keeps pace with this (Cranfield Institute).[iv]

Here are some more insights from our research study based on over 600 small businesses that I think you'll find useful.

Face to face activity is very important to most people – either selling or meeting one to one or networking at traditional networking events. Most spent about 2-4 hours a week networking face to face and less than 1 hour on line.

However a minority spent a lot of time on line – over 8 hours.

And we found that 40% of the people who spent more than 8 hours on line also spent more than 8 hours face to face – and vice versa. In fact we have consistently found that those who make the online media work best for them are also good face to face networkers.

It's as if they're designing the scenery for their own play. They could still hold the play without the scenery. **But good scenery is worth a 40% uplift in enquiries – and so ultimately sales.**

What they're doing is consciously building their reputation. You could too.

Reputation depends on

> knowing your stuff,
> being competent in delivery
> and being easy to work with

Being successful means having lots of people who know these things about you. And creating and maintaining relationships with those crucial 50 people who are going to use and recommend your services.

In the networked economy it's not who you know that's important – it's who knows you. And it's not what you know – it's what they know that you know.

That's why we spent so much time banging on about "What's your story?"

Before we go into the detail of what marketing looks like in this strange new landscape, we need another interlude – one that looks at how networks operate.

How networks function

In today's world it's ever more important to understand how networks operate.

People have always worked in networks – typically there are 2 approaches, one is to associate with a small group that supports you. This is traditional operating. The family works like this in Asian (or Italian!) communities. Modern versions like BNI and BRX work this way – a small tight knit group of individuals who meet regularly and share leads and breakfast.

However there have always been other types of networkers who join these close-knit groups. They have lots of weak ties to people and fulfil the "friend of a friend" role that brings in random, unexpected opportunities. Granovetter found that most job opportunities come through exactly this kind of weak tie. [v]

However if you dig into this you find that not all networkers are created equal. The defining experiment was carried out by Stanley Milgram who established the 6 steps theory – that we are all connected to everyone in the world through 6 other people. He tested this by giving a letter addressed to an individual in New York to several hundred people and asked them to send this letter on a friend- of a friend basis to see what routes they took. [vi]

It turns out that the vast majority connected to this person through just 3 individuals.

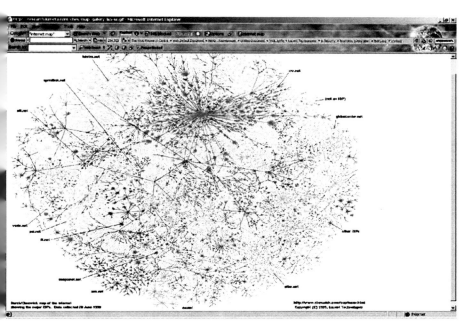

This is the Lucent internet map. It shows the guiding principle that networks are lumpy, uneven. Some nodes are much more connected than others with many connections while most have very few.

These are the points that lots of traffic goes through. In the traditional world sales agents are like this – they know lots of people and use their connection to do deals and generate money.

It's the same off-line – some people are just much more known and connected than others. You can see this in blogs. Here's the blogosphere (☺) as seen by Technorati which shows the power of blogs invading the traditional news network domains. What this says is that there are a mighty few and a million also-rans.

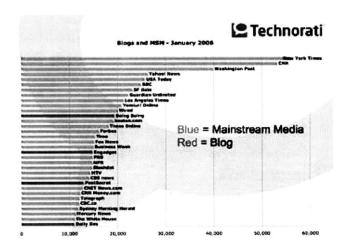

Does this remind you of Geoffrey Moore, the Gorillas and the Monkeys – it should. We find the same patterns occurring in networks, markets and anywhere that people make a free-ish choice about what they do, read or whom they associate with. And it's from these super-connected individuals that at least some of your top 50 people should be drawn.

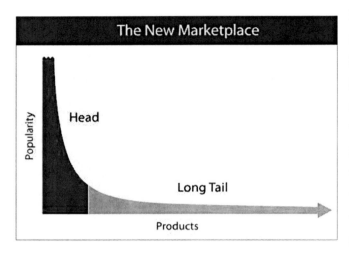

For the scientists among you it's called Zipf's law. What this says is that the second player in a market has half the market share of the number 1 player, the third has a third, the quarter has a quarter etc. If for the sake of argument we say that the leader has a 40% share then the number 2 has 20%, the number 3 has 16% and the number 4 has 10%.

These are the chimps – after that you're in monkey territory. This means you have to decide as part of your business strategy whether you are going to play in the fat-head or the long tail. I know we've said it already but it's important!

So if you're a blogger you're going to decide whether to be Boing Boing or Craigslist or whether you're going to demonstrate your expertise by knowing a lot about a little.

The same is true of networks. Here are the top 6 UK networkers on Ecademy in 2008 – a social networking site. (I was number 95 in the UK with around 1130 at that time)

Name	Organization and Location	Network size
Thomas Power Ecademy London UK		18728
Jim Tuffin http://www.jtuffin.co.uk Southampton Hampshire UK		10560
Geoff Cox Business over Breakfast , Birmingham		6436
Denis Kondopoulos Naxtech.com Reading Berkshire UK		3485
r i c h a r d p e r r y Maidenhead Berkshire UK		3451
Andrew Widgery Business Scene Ltd Haslemere Surrey UK		3433

So as you can see the theory is supported in that the pattern holds in the data.

Thomas Power of Ecademy is the polar extreme from organisations like BNI and BRE. He maintains that quantity of connections is all-important - that the money is in the connections not the nodes. Clearly as the head of a networking organisation it works for him. He advocates an open and random approach to networking.

Let's dig a bit deeper.

As we said earlier, one of the challenges of networking is to strike the right balance between focused and targeted networking and Ecademy is good at delivering measured amounts of randomness. It's method of connection is essentially random. But what's unique about http://www.Ecademy.com is that it effectively supports both online and off-line networking.

http://www.linkedin.com by contrast is completely purposeful. It essentially maps your first 3 circles of connectedness and lets you plan a route of introductions to whoever you are trying to reach / sell to. Then you can ask your network for introductions and you will be passed on or not according to the strength of your reputation. We'll discuss this in more detail later.

So making use of a network, small or large, involves aligning with and getting to know the most connected members – and getting them to trust you so that they will pass your ideas or opportunities on.

However there is a taxonomy of these individuals. Some are essentially salesmen, some just like connecting people, and some are subject experts – mavens in the terminology used by Malcolm Gladwell in his book, "The Tipping Point". [vii]

So you need to be clear what you're doing in the network – are you selling, looking for advocates, employees or finance – or are you just trying to get ideas spread – the individuals chosen to work with will be different in each case.

You may need to consider incentives if you are to truly motivate them to amplify your own activities. In Seth Godin's useful book "Unleashing the Idea Virus" he identifies either money or kudos as motivators for highly connected individuals. (It looks like we're back to the usual triangle of fear, greed and fashion here.)[viii]

So reputation is functioning as a personal brand. It brings you a dividend over and above the connections you can make by your own efforts.

Within this networked environment, our research shows that people recommend other people that they understand what they do, that get back to them quickly, who have a good reputation and who are known to perform. They also prefer people who engage, who listen and who take the time to build relationships. That's why the old, transactional, interruption marketing model is losing ground all the time.

Cialdini in his book "Influence - Science and Practice" identifies the principle of reciprocation as one of the cornerstones of building strong human relationships. This underlies the principle of Givers Gain or paying it forward that is so much at the basis of much networking philosophy.[ix]

Other key characteristics he mentions are Commitment and Consistency, Social Proof, Liking, Authority and Scarcity. This is all summarised in his book "Influence – Science and Practice" which is a must for anyone serious about building a successful business presence.

If you can build and maintain a good reputation for competence in a sought after area and are generally pleasant to deal with, networking is a great way of leveraging your ability to reach more customers.

Our research found that commitment and consistency were very important criteria for being referred.

And that's why it's crucial to be absolutely clear about what you do because being consistent is a key part of building a good reputation as is.

Being easy to talk to

Listening a lot

Finding helpful connections for the other person.

You also have to be clear about what you want from networking – be it collaborators, referrals, employees, introductions to finance. If you are helpful and you let other people know clearly what you do and what you want, consistently – then the magic will start to occur.

Social proof is another concept that's really important in understanding how networks operate. If enough other people think you're important and interesting then you must be. Hence the popularity of giving and receiving testimonials in environments like Ecademy and Linked-in and the importance of the re-Tweet button on twitter – you're effectively handing out social proof to those you value and/or like.

Being liked is pivotal. Alas for some of us, looking good is important to being liked. But if you're not naturally beautiful you can at least be well turned out, hold yourself well and try and appear symmetrical.

Finally, we found that the process of building trust – givers gain / responsiveness / good reputation / consistent positive attitude established by reputation and one to one meetings are valued by all types, sizes and styles of company. So time spent using these behaviours to establish a clear, positive reputation is clearly a sound investment.

As a final summary to this section here are two lists – one is Cialdini's list of things that attract attention and exert influence. The other is the list of traits that our research respondents value in fellow networkers.[x]

Cialdini's List

- Contrast
- Reciprocation
- Surprise
- Consistency
- Writing it out or saying it makes it true
- Social Proof
- Liking
- Symmetry
- Association with good things
- Scarcity / time limits

Our respondents value people

- who do what they say
- who know their subject
- with a can do attitude
- who will commit
- who respond quickly
- Who follow up referrals
- who do good work
- Who deliver on their promises
- Who have a good reputation
- Who are clear about what they do, who they are targeting and what value they add
- Who listen
- Who understand the principle of Giver's Gain

Building your marketing plan

Here's what the SMEs from our 2009 survey actually did to promote themselves.

Technique	Use regularly %	Depend on it %	Total %
One to One selling	43.4	30.8	74.2
Social Networks	50.1	21.6	71.7
Workshops	23.6	6.6	30.2
PR	21.8	7.5	29.3
Online advertising	22.6	4.9	27.5
Email Shots	23.5	3.2	26.7
Newsletters	22.2	2.2	24.4
Direct Mail	18.6	3	21.6
Blogs	14.1	3.7	17.8
Print advertising	13.4	1.4	14.8
Telesales	12	2.7	14.7
Exhibitions	8.9	0.9	9.8
E-zines	5	1.4	6.4
Leaflet Drops	4.4	1.5	5.9

This sample (largely recruited from BNI and Ecademy members) prefer face to face activities to on-line activities. However Linked-In ranks high and has become an important environment for smaller businesses. This may be because professional bodies such as the Chartered Institute of Marketing and the Institute of Directors have now created online communities here.

Larger organisations tend to use telemarketing more but it's surprising how little use is made of leaflet drops – even amongst targeted local businesses. The main offline tools turn out to workshops, PR and (to a limited extent) direct mail. Here are the most popular networking environments.

	Don't or occasional use %	Use regularly or depend %
BNI	47.7	53.2
Other face to face events	61.9	38.6
Linked-in	69.8	30.2
Ecademy	70.7	29.9
Chamber of commerce events	74.2	25.8
Professional body events	82.5	17.5
Facebook	84.5	15.7
exhibitions	88.2	12.3
Twitter	92.8	7.2

Twitter has a comparatively high ranking as an online tool given that it is both new and relatively tech-y. (If it was measured now we believe it would be much higher) BNI and Ecademy are of course highly placed since that was the source of the bulk of the respondents. Facebook was not highly rated. However more recently it has become important for B2C marketing with 12% of Sales for online retail originating there. [xi]

US companies and BNI members seem to use electronic networks relatively less frequently while networks that combine online and offline networking opportunities appeal to European companies, companies with between 3 and 20 employees and those who favour other online networks.

We investigated the size of networking groups that people favoured and found that over half of the individuals surveyed favoured a networking group of between 21 and 40 with the mode value (31.5%) between 21 and 30.

So it seems that individuals like to get to know a core group of people well with whom they can collaborate and refer business – and for a local business that may be all that they need.

Preferred Size of core networking groups.

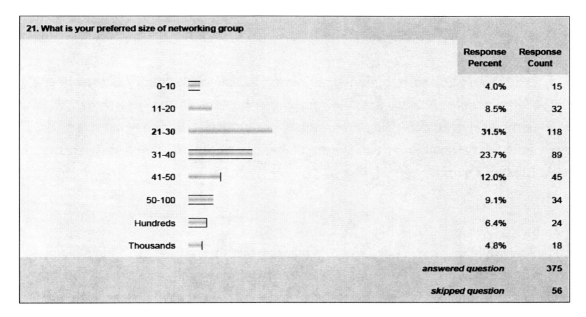

21. What is your preferred size of networking group	Response Percent	Response Count
0-10	4.0%	15
11-20	8.5%	32
21-30	31.5%	118
31-40	23.7%	89
41-50	12.0%	45
50-100	9.1%	34
Hundreds	6.4%	24
Thousands	4.8%	18
answered question		375
skipped question		56

The table shows that the presence of a small core group as a home base for support and referrals is a very common requirement for the small business owner and is particularly favoured by non-scalable, local businesses and those not so keen on networking at all. Interestingly enough the size of the home group approaches the "overnight stop" version of the Dunbar Number which is 38.

Robin Dunbar is Professor of Evolutionary Anthropology at the University of Oxford. He spent his formative research years studying how primates interact and the role of grooming in building networks and tribes. [xii]

He came to several interesting conclusions that have become well publicised (if less well understood) in the world of networking.

One conclusion is that language evolved since it makes it easier to build bonds instead of all that grooming – it's about 3.8 times as effective – because the optimum sized conversation group is 3.8. (If you study restaurant bookings you will discover that the average number that tables are booked for is ….3.8!

This has allowed humans to build bigger networks. Dunbar's theory is that keeping track of the people we know and their networks has driven the growth of the brain particularly the neo-cortex. However, Dunbar believes that there is an upper limit to the number of relationships you can model of around 150. This is called Dunbar's number

You will often hear people say Dunbar's number means that we can't have more than that number of relationships. However this is not really the case. It in fact represents not only your connections with them but their connections with each other. In order to know how individuals will respond in different conditions you need to know how they see each other. Empirically the military over thousands of years from the Romans to the present day operate in tactical units of about 120 and it also represents the optimal size of a village – or a business.

Individuals who prefer much larger groups often seem to be promoting a scalable business on a national or global scale. Larger groups are popular amongst larger, European companies and Ecademists as well as high growth and global companies. The Dunbar tribal number is 1155 so it would be interesting to speculate as to whether this is the optimal size for a tribe "led" around a particular idea. Could you create and lead a niche of this size? **If so what would you call it? Write it here.**

Academic research into networks suggests that a business owner with an open network with diverse connections (i.e. many weak ties and social connections) will have greater opportunities to develop a successful business than someone with many connections in a single/closed network.

A closed network lacks the bridges where one person links two separate but dense networks. These gaps allow 'networking brokers' to link different networks together by transferring information or resources and facilitating the interests of people not otherwise directly related. Understanding how these brokers operate, identifying and including them in our "gang of 50" would be part of the strategy of someone trying to build a scalable, national or international business.

However there is more to this than just numbers and spotting who the well connected nodes are. There is also the issue of the topology or shape of the network. The way knowledge (or diseases if we are an epidemiologist) spreads through a network depends on the shape of the network and our position in it. Networks that have dense clusters of well connected people centrally positioned spread information quickly to those centrally. Groups on the periphery don't get the information so rapidly and may be at a competitive disadvantage.

Research into the way that weak ties operate suggests that most opportunities come from people in the second or third tier of people who know you. Friends of Friends.

 Mapping these networks in detail is time consuming and really requires computing power and dedicated algorithms. However you can start to make some headway in working out what's going on further out in your network via Friend of a Friend files (FOAF) so that you can see who knows who. You can do this in social networking sites or find out who knows a given individual using FOAF tools like http://semantictweet.com/

More useful is to have a snapshot of who is communicating with whom. Within the twitter world tools like mention map will give you a clue. http://apps.asterisq.com/mentionmap, essentially maps what topics and conversations a particular individual has had on twitter in the last 24 hours. It's good for tracking who is talking to whom and current topics of interest – at least among the twitterati. Not so useful if you're stalking the sale of a part of an aero-engine with Rolls-Royce.

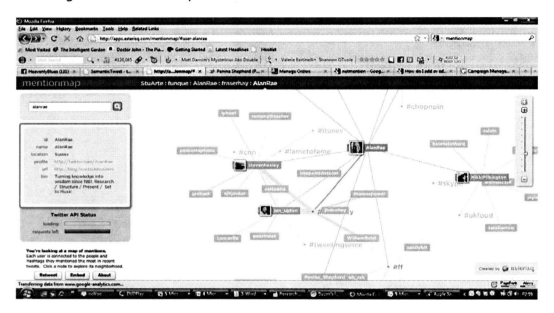

This can give you a way of informing yourself about who it might be worthwhile communicating with – however, it's only as good as your real world presence if you are seeking to use it commercially.

Still, the online world gives you an easy way of re-instating and maintaining weak ties with a far greater number of people than you could manage conventionally. These individuals are unlikely to buy from you directly – but their friends and friends of friends might – if you are clear about what you do when you re-contact them via Facebook or Linked-In

In their book "connected", Nicholas Christakis and James Fowler review how networks operate. One of their conclusions was that online marketing delivers four new characteristics over the traditional methods.

Enormity – you can build and maintain much bigger networks

Communality – you can become known within a grouping

Specificity – you can identify key people you want to contact

Virtuality – you can do it all from your back bedroom

However this still begs the question of whether your networking should be targeted and specific or whether there is value in connecting randomly and seeing what happens. [xiii]

The "Ecademy viewpoint" stresses the importance of a Random, supportive and open approach to networking. [xiv]So we considered the role of chance in business during our networking research project– we asked people what importance they attached to randomness – the results were interesting. We've identified that most online networking environments (apart from Linked-in) are quite random in the way they permit connections.

Groups that were more pro-chance than average were Linked-in and Ecademy users and UK and European companies. Groups that were less open to chance encounters were BNI and US members, companies employing more than 20, older people, people who plan and those who avoid online networking and whose businesses have a local focus.

Does this have any significance? Does it relate to a preference for large networking groups and those who are heavy online networkers? What's the underlying logic and under what circumstances do these characteristics and activities deliver an advantage?

After a lot of time spent punishing the data we think we know the answer. We've previously studied characteristics of early adopters of the internet for marketing and operational / collaboration purposes. How did they differ from the large number of small, local, on-line avoiders that we found in the sample? How did our gifted amateurs who wanted to stay small but have a wide reach and manage growth through collaboration differ from businesses following a conventional business growth path?

We divided our sample as to whether their business was local (80% of their business coming from within a 50 mile radius) or national /global on one axis.

And whether the business was scalable (based on their own assessment of whether they were held back by people and systems constraints or whether they were held back by lack of orders).

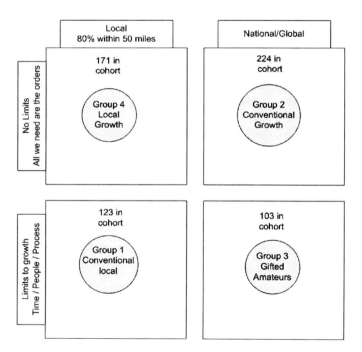

This gave us 4 groups whose sizes are shown in the diagram. The labels of conventional local, local growth and conventional growth explain themselves. The gifted amateurs are characterised by being IT skilled but who tend to use cloud based techniques to avoid growing a conventional infrastructure. Lisa Harris and I named the "Gifted Amateurs" in one of our papers.[xv]

We looked at the attitudes of each of these groups to chance, to their use of electronic media and their use of local, small networking groups like BNI.

For once in our lives, the answers were quite clear cut. As you can see – it's not the scalability that makes the difference to company online behaviour but whether the business sees itself as local or not.

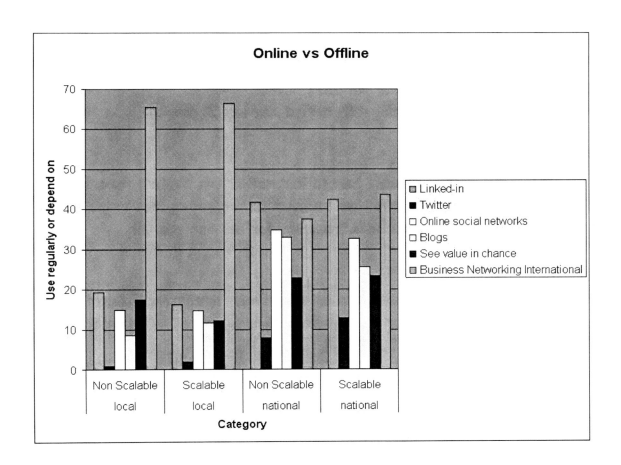

National businesses, whether scalable or non scalable were twice as likely to use online tools such as Linked In Twitter online social networks or Blogs. They're also significantly more likely to value randomness in business.

So what this all means is that if you have a local business – you can probably find your key 50 people by networking locally.

The BNI model seems popular – but so is going to meetings organised by local chambers of commerce or professional bodies. This doesn't mean you can do without a web presence or even a Blog. But it's probably going to be scenery. The real action will be face to face.

If you want to reach a global or national audience – chances are you will need to use the electronic media intelligently to find your key 50 people.

But you will still need to do some face to face networking. In fact the only networking group that seems to have a mechanism for leading from online connections to face to face ones is Ecademy – for two main reasons.

Firstly its structures and facilities allow and promote much more in depth conversations that the rather shallow interactions supported by Linked In and Facebook.

And crucially it organises and promotes face to face meetings of various sizes ranging from one to one meetings via boardrooms of 10-12 individuals up to the London meetings which may be attended by several hundred people.

Building and supporting your online presence.

To be successful online you need to learn how to build a strong online presence by being active, being seen to be responsive and getting used to using keywords to leave signposts back to a site that allows generating enquiries and capturing details of people interested in your offers.

You might want to set up a system that offers a free download – such as a marketing or gardening planner in exchange for permission to follow up via a newsletter subscription for example. It's quite easy to arrange this via email managing clients such as www.Mailchimp.co.uk which is the one I use.

Going this route will benefit you since it makes sure that your list is fully compliant with the regulatory authorities and you are unlikely to get blacklisted which is an increasing issue for the amateur emailer. And it's an inexpensive way of generating site traffic and building an email list.

Whatever story you tell on the site should be backed up by a few white papers, slide sets, articles, photographs and videos all properly tagged for maximum effect.

Finally you should become confident in using workshops and PR. Preparing these lets you continually hone, define and develop your copywriting skills for emails, blogs and articles.

> Our central insight in this book is that online activity is largely the scenery for a play that takes place in the real world. You need to construct a unique balance of structured and random activity to deliver an effective business model that both builds business relationships and allows transactions to occur

.

Open, random activity is about relationships, building trust and creating opportunities. Closed and selective activity is about transactions and follow up to deliver an effective, consistent result to your customers.

Only you can decide on that balance.

Brand is about performance but you may need some randomness in connections at the opening stage of the sale. The advantage of environments like Ecademy and Twitter is that you can inject a known amount of randomness into your business model according to how much time you spend there.

So if you need 20% random activity in your business model – spend 20% of your sales and marketing time in "random" spaces like Ecademy and twitter.

Now it's time to decide which techniques we should be using.

Conventional marketing wisdom says that it takes 7 interactions of various kinds before an individual buys something. Most companies give up after 3 contacts – so it's not surprising that many companies don't get the results they should.

Perseverance furthers – as it says in the I Ching[xvi]

The marketing options vary. As well as the online approaches we've talked about, Face to face techniques include networking, traditional selling, exhibitions and workshops – both of which can be very powerful for building your company's credibility with suppliers as well as customers.

Written approaches include direct mail, PR, blogging, literature and the web-site itself.

Then there is conventional advertising in a variety of media plus the use of pay per click advertising – which combined with the free download of useful information, has slashed the cost of generating qualified leads from £30 in the mid 90s to under £1 today.

So how do you decide what you should be doing?

As we discussed earlier, there's a clear distinction between businesses which systematically benefit from a wider platform and those that won't

Most businesses need a balance between closed, purposeful, activity and open, chance driven activity and this varies as we've discussed.

As there is a lot of random, international activity on social business sites, they can be used to inject some necessary randomness into the business model.

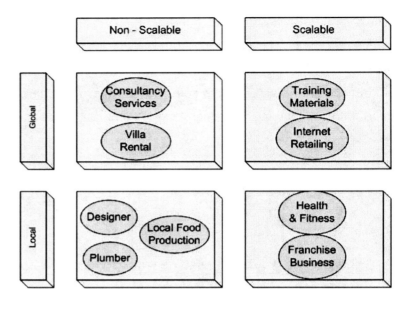

It can be controlled by the amount of time spent on line. Here are some examples of where different types of businesses can be expected to sit within this matrix

So let's see where you sit on these continuums

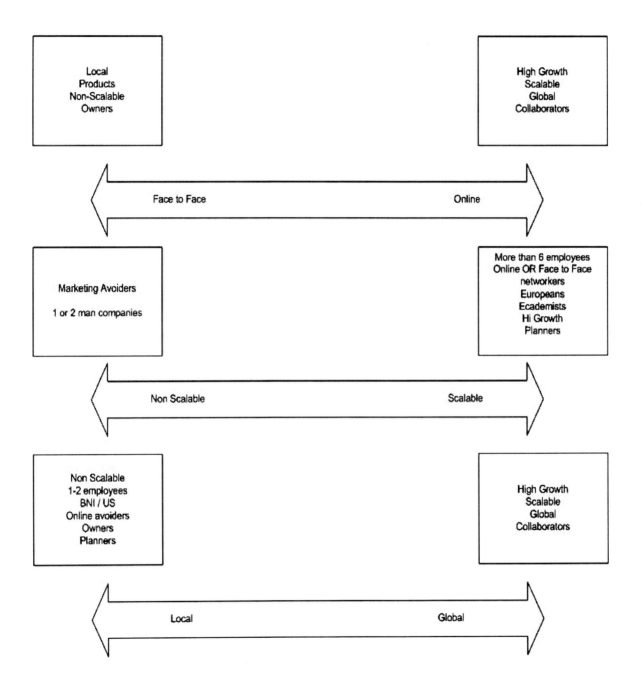

Do I need an Online or a real world Focus?

Be reassured. It's not an either or choice. The best online networkers are also good at face to face. 40% of people who spent more than 8 hours a week online networking also spent 8 hours a week face to face. And vice versa. Apart from being keen at it they have a good reason.

If you are running a scalable business that's not bounded by a local catchment area, then it's likely that you will need to build up a wide ranging number of contacts – particularly looking for those who have a large number of contacts themselves.

There is benefit in a lot of random connections but there is more in getting close to the key influencers. If you know where to look you can find out who they are – and if you can deliver a consistent, scalable product or service – then you can really start to leverage yourself out of the long tail and into the fat head.

However to play there, what you deliver is truly world class and that means focus on operations. Because it's delivering repeatable, good experiences that will build your brand.

You have 12.5 hours per week – what will you do?

The techniques that your fellow networkers favour for generating leads and sales are overwhelmingly one to one selling and social networks of the kind we've talked about. Following on from these, the next most popular tools are

Workshops

PR

Online advertising

Email Shots

Newsletters

These are all media where you are interacting directly with your customers, either face to face or in writing. This is why we spend so much time on getting your story right – and concise.

Working online is very good for your skills. If you use Google ad-words you have a 25 character headline and two x 35 character sentences to get your message across. If you use twitter you have 140 characters. The discipline of using these tools will help you promote yourself much more effectively and we'll focus on these in the practical section of our workbook.

Our survey suggested that there was a limited appetite for online marketing mainly because nearly 40% of those surveyed were running local businesses or were 1 or 2 man businesses delivering business services – so generally not scalable. So this may not apply to you at all.

If you are selling products or have a scalable business it's really valuable to have an effective on line strategy.

The 24% of our respondees that spent more than 6 hours networking on line per week mainly used

Linked In	30.2%
Ecademy	29.2%
Blogs	17.6%
Facebook	15.7%
Twitter	7.2%

Online media become more important as traditional intrusive marketing approaches become unusable. We see references to a "response crunch". And there is growing legislative backlash against unsolicited communications of all kinds – both in the US and in the European Union. This applies not only to emails but also to unsolicited phone and fax approaches.

One way of getting round this is to build an online reputation and to get people to notice, connect with you and voluntarily listen to what you have to say. Online media allow you to tackle this in different ways.

To connect on linked-in – you must know them already, share a previous connection or be introduced. On twitter they take a positive decision to follow you. Ecademy is more open – but people can still choose to ignore you.

But the same basic strategies and behaviours apply on line as offline.

Identify the structure of the space you're in and connect with the most connected

Listen before you speak

When you do speak be clear about what you stand for

Remember that people are as interested in you as in your product

Always remember this is about dialogue not broadcasting a controlled message – probably why the corporates hate it.

And finally follow the principle of givers gain.

The role of your web-site / web presence

Your web-site is the hub of the wheel of your marketing. It might be better to describe it as your primary web presence.

This could be a blog, a profile on linked-in or Facebook or even a twitter ID. As we move to a web of information streams from a web of static pages and where approaching 30% of internet interactions are mobile (37% in the case of twitter) then it's important to have the options covered.

It gives you a shop window, a space to deliver social proof and a way to get people to contact and interact with you.

It's the scenery for the play of your networking. In 2011 people Google you – before meeting you formally and after meeting you when networking. When they type your name in to Google you want them to find good entries – leading to a clean, professional web presence with a call to action.

Until recently Google was the winner of the search wars. However it is rapidly being caught up by Facebook searches and Twitter is increasingly taking a slice of the search action – given that it operates in real time. As of December 2010, Facebook has overtaken Google as the most visited site.

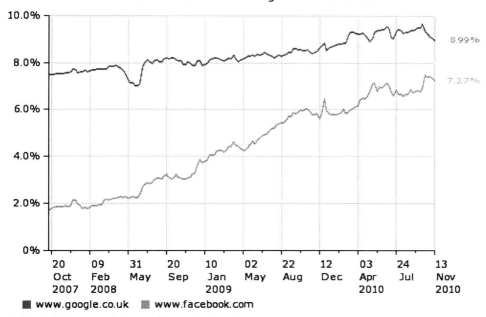

UK Internet Visits to Google and Facebook

■ www.google.co.uk ■ www.facebook.com

Weekly market share in 'All Categories', measured by visits, based on UK usage.
Created: 15/11/2010. © Copyright 1996-2010 Hitwise Pty. Ltd.   Source: Experian Hitwise UK

Your web presence can be seen as a step in a sales process. It needs to be easy to find – and once the customer is there it needs to arouse their hopes or their fears and lead them to take action. You want them to

    Buy something now
    Download or read some proof that you are as good as you say
    Contact you now.
    En gage with you in a conversation

Your web-site helps you automate the prospecting part of your sales activity to deliver a string of warm, part qualified leads. How you do this is different in different business situations. If you are selling products nationally and scalably you take a different approach from someone selling a local personal or business service. But the principle's the same.

You are going to drive traffic by one of 3 routes

Written materials – from PR and white papers to blogs and tweets

Networking and conversations - online or offline

Advertising via affiliate links, Google ad-words and other paid links.

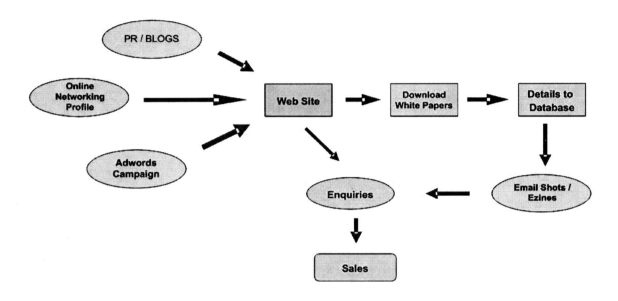

And when they're there you want customers to either buy something directly - or ring you up – or download some kind of proof of competence – a free, useful tool that fulfils the requirements of giver's gain.

Driving traffic by networking

Networking includes face to face activity and social media. In face to face networking, you meet people and they check you out on line. This is particularly noticeable in business services, supply chains or other more traditional businesses.

Online you can use social media networking sites like linked-in, Ecademy, Facebook. They include hosted promotional platforms like BT Tradespace or Squidoo and Blogging tools like WordPress and Blogger as well as micro-blogging tools like Twitter.

Use these tools cleverly and you can greatly expand the reach of your ideas and your brand without spending much money. It can however be time-consuming.

If you have a scalable business where you can sell all over the country or even the world, then it's a very cheap and effective way of extending your reach and getting your ideas relayed.

People who are good at it are spending over 8 hours a week at it. The top web-informed 20% of our sample are doing just that. AND you have to be more transparent, open and honest than is normal in traditional, command and control organisations. This is why the corporates often struggle to understand and resist taking part in social media.

This is a real break with tradition in communication. Most of us grew up in a world where the flow of information was controlled by big organisations that set the agenda and told us what they wanted us to know.

By contrast, in the web 2.0 world, there is a free competition of ideas and something like 12% of participants are actively creating the content that informs those active on the net.

Research shows that people trust people like themselves as the most reliable source of information. The fact that there IS so much competition means that the consensus view about FACTUAL things is generally the right one. It's like a big "ask the audience". So we work really hard to keep our Amazon reputation really good for our www.theintelligentgarden.com business

The power of trust is seen in things like Wikipedia – an encyclopaedia created by volunteers collaboratively - which is generally reckoned to be as accurate as the professionally produced Encyclopaedia Britannica. Certainly there are contentious areas such as the Middle East – but these are flagged as such.

Replication and Leverage

For the new social media marketer, the beauty is that you write something in one place and have it appear in various other places. Something written in a Blog can be piped into Ecademy and Facebook profiles, can appear in a Squidoo lens and can be broadcast to your own opt-in followers via twitter.

That's illustrated in the following diagram

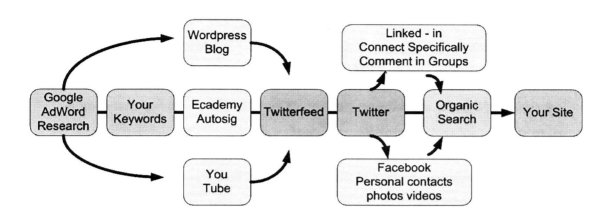

We'll tell you how to set this up in Part 2.

You can start with a low level Adwords campaign to establish the keywords that you can use for search engine optimisation and tagging.

You can Blog on Ecademy or use it's marketplace to get the benefit of improving organic search. And on WordPress to build your own source of reference material. These can be consolidated into articles and put on sites like ezine articles and article base or used to create slide sets to share on www.slideshare.net

Your toolkit should definitely include a linked-in profile for targeting connections and possibly a face book profile for more personal connections. If you are selling product or performances, a FaceBook fan page is an important addition to your armoury. Recent research shows that getting on for 20% of online purchases start life from links out from Facebook pages – driven by people talking to their friends.

Try to include some you-tube videos and photos on Flickr to add interest– tagged so that people will find you and link back to your site.

And you will want some activity on twitter to spread the word far and wide.

We're going to cover the basics of these tools and how to use them effectively without it taking over your life in the rest of this book.

Most of this is free. Even Ecademy is only £10 per month. And you can do it with much less work than you think. All of these social medial tools are already set up to use RSS (really simple syndication) which effectively carries out the plumbing for you outlined in the earlier diagram so that information created in one place can be routed to somewhere else on the internet.

You can write some good materials on your Blog and automatically route it to your Facebook or other profile. You can also send the feed to a feed aggregator like Twitterfeed which will allow all of your content to be transmitted to people who've chosen to follow your ideas automatically. This is a good way of promoting your ideas and offers.

And you can automate the production and dissemination of it.

BUT THERE'S A CATCH

To be accepted as a thought leader on line, you have to follow the principles of networking. You wouldn't go into a networking situation with your megaphone and start telling the world about your current offer. So don't do it on line.

This is not about broadcasting – it's about conversations and reciprocation. Listen first, and then join in. Make sure what you say is sensible and interesting and relates to the pre-occupations of your listeners. Build a bit of a reputation, do a few favours and then you can start introducing some of your own stuff.

But you're networkers – you know all this. Just behave the same way and everything will be fine. You don't have arguments with people in a networking situation – so don't do it on line.

Being

      Helpful

      Interesting

      Informative

      Supportive

Is what will build your reputation, get you referred and allow you to promote yourself in a collaborative kind of way.

The same rules work on-line as off-line. People give business with people they like who have a good reputation for doing that kind of work. And don't say anything that would embarrass you in front of your granny.

2 Things you need to remember about the internet

It's verbal – words drive searches – and links.
And words drive branding

In the offline world we want to own phrases in the customers' mind. Online we want to own them in Google's mind also. So that's why after we brainstorm the keywords that people use to find them we test them in Adwords to validate which ones win.

Then you can use them as tags for blogs, for headlines, first paragraphs and title tags on your web pages (aka DIY search engine optimisation) and as anchor text in your auto signatures on Ecademy and in inbound links for your site.

Over time this means that your organic search rankings for the optimised sites will start to rise. Over time this will result in you attracting more potential clients for the goods and services you offer.

In parallel with this you want to build a strong online presence that will bring us additional attention from well connected players who can refer us.

So what are the key tools you can use?

Blogging tools - WordPress

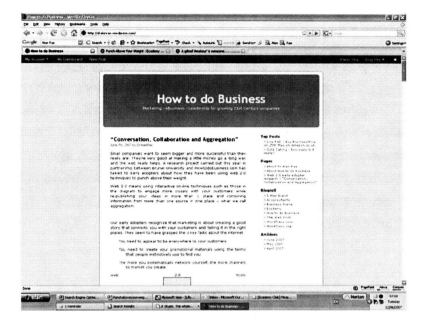

We have standardized on WordPress as our blogging tool because

It's easy to use

It integrates with your own site

You can create additional static pages so it functions as mini-site

It's customizable

The tagging is foolproof

You can link to other sites via your blogroll.

WordPress exists in 2 flavours, .com and .org. The .com version which we use for www.HowtodoBusiness.com and www.PunchaboveyourWeight.com is hosted by WordPress has all the things in it you need and you can just set up and go.

We used the .org version on recent sites like www.theintelligentgarden.com and www.growingjobs.org. It's downloadable and you have to do more work with it and host it yourself. The good news is you can be as commercial with it as you like while the .com version will penalize you if you overly "commercial". The best route is to host the domain name with a hosting company that allows a one-click installation. I have had good results with www.justhost.com. Once installed you can choose from one of many themes to structure your content for you. I have used Atahualpa a lot and found it flexible and attractive.

It's very easy to set up and use and can be considered as a cornerstone of your on-line activity. If you are running a business services company, a Blog can be an ideal business tool as long as you can generate 300 - 400 words of well written copy every 7-10 days.

As well as being used for external communication, you can also use blogs within a business too. Service businesses, once they grow past a certain point, need to focus on internal branding to keep their own team on message. A company Blog is one tool for doing this.

Social Media

There are many social networking sites that you can join but the most important for practical purposes are these. Linked-in was definitely considered the most important by our interviewees (although there were many Ecademy users, they formed a large part of the recruitment cohort). As you can see they vary quite considerably in the way they are used – and the social etiquette that is used on each platform.

	Ecademy	Facebook	Linked-In
Connection Mechanism	Look at profile - ask to connect	Ask to connect	Ask to connect if you know them. Get introduced if you don't
Can you see profile of someone you're not connected with	Yes	No	Yes
Primary Use	Business + Social	Social	Business
Typical User	Small Business	Individual	Corporate
Connection Style	Random	Amongst Friends	Deliberate
Groups and Clubs	yes	yes	Yes
Rich Media Friendly	A bit	Yes	No

Ecademy

Ecademy is one of the smaller networking sites but it's a good place to start –the subscription is £10 per month. While it allows you to network online and offline with 100,000 other members worldwide (6,000 of which are active). It also lets you

> Create blogs
> Advertise in the Market Place
> Form special interest clubs
> Take part in discussions, seek advice from other members or give advice in response to the posts of others

If you devote time to learning to use it – it really is a school of online marketing.

There are 2 unique features which make Ecademy important:

It runs face to face meetings as well as supporting online networking. So you can meet potential referees and collaborators and set up one to ones more effectively than you would in a pure online situation like on Facebook.

There is so much user created content on Ecademy that Google looks at it every day and anything you post there, if you have optimised your autosignature properly will deliver a search engine linking bonus. Every time you Blog on the Ecademy front page, an interested reader's click on your autosignature boosts your Google profile. The more interactive the discussion the more opportunity for click backs and the more your brand profile is raised.

In addition to the SEO advantage of using Ecademy intelligently, there is the issue that the content has some really interesting information in its own right. In fact, I have recently been analysing my own online networks and it's only really on Ecademy that I have made new, valuable and lasting contacts. Pretty much everyone I'm connected with on Facebook or Linked-in are either people I know in the real world or I had met via Ecademy first.

You can have a comprehensive profile – with embedded YouTube video and although it takes time to learn to drive, it definitely has a pivotal role in an online marketing strategy. It will let you contact all of your connections that you have made once a month. Or members of any clubs you have set up.

Facebook

Facebook originated as a Harvard student project and now has 30 million members world-wide. It's a social networking platform that welcomes external applications. It blurs boundaries between 'professional' and 'social' worlds. This can be fine if you live a blameless life. You can also guarantee that publishing your email address will generate spam beyond your wildest dreams. Many people choose to keep it purely social.

Can it be used for business applications effectively?

Special interest groups can be created on relevant topics. See for example, 'Facebook for Business' or indeed "How to do Business" which seems to have acquired 600 members with very little energy being applied. RSS feeds can pull in content from your Blog or other source – a special WordPress application allows basic Blog management from within Facebook.

Facebook Flyers can be accessed from the 'advertisers' section at the bottom of your profile page. The flyer can create localised awareness that can be targeted to individual locations. The message may be all text or include a small photo or graphic element.

If you want to reach people from Generation Y as employees or customers it may be worth spending some time with it.

It's particularly good for allowing other people to build applications to run within it and has done very well with easily importing pictures and videos

You can contact all your contacts and members of any groups that you have set up.

Recently, however, the game seems to have changed considerably. Facebook has just (January 2011) overtaken Google as the most visited site.

According to Robin Goad's brilliant blog "Hitwise Intelligence" , here in the UK, it's now second only to Google in terms of visits and vastly swamps anything else in terms of pages viewed. In September it received 16.4% of all page views in the UK. That's of ALL of them. It also accounted for 7.27% of all visits in the last period – only being pipped at the post by Google with 8.99%

It now has 55% of the visits for social networks – with YouTube the next player at 16% and it accounts for nearly 10% of ongoing traffic to sites making it the second most important source of traffic after Google. This figure rises to 12% for online retail sites.

So if you haven't got a FaceBook strategy or at least a fan page yet – maybe you should be thinking about it. We have used fan pages successfully with The Intelligent Garden and Plants4Presents.

Linked-in

Linked-in is the most transactional of the social media networks. Thomas Power of Ecademy describes it as networking American Style.

You create a profile in the same way – but it's much more structured and targeted. You can only connect with people directly if you already know them (or at least their email address).

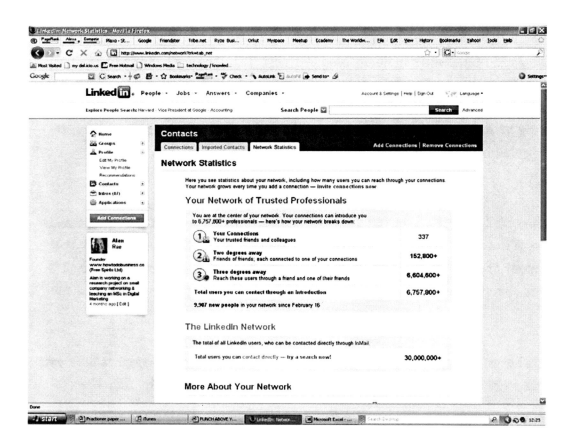

It works very much on the basis of levels of connection. You have a first circle of people that you are directly connected to, a 2nd circle of their connections and a

3rd circle of their connections. You have access to these people but only by invitation.

If I want to connect to a specific individual I can search for something like "Google vice president" This will produce a list of people. There is one who's a senior programmer in Krakow. Apparently 14 people who know me know someone who knows him. If I want to contact him I send one of my contacts a message saying why I want to get in contact with him and ask them to pass the request on via their contacts. If everyone feels comfortable I get an introduction to him and we can connect.

It's used a lot by people who are recruiting or doing structured selling particularly into or out of the corporate sector. So its connection criteria are strict. You should only connect with people that you know well so that you can refer them with some degree of integrity.

This is quite different from the situation in Ecademy where you can easily make totally random connections with anyone or Facebook where you can easily search the networks of people you already know and ask to connect to anyone that looks interesting.

However the reason that it has become the online networking tool of choice for our sample is because as well as finding specific people you can join groups where you can get known by asking and answering questions and so find your key 50 players in a systematic way.

If you are trying to recruit individuals for a specific event, or get people to reply to a questionnaire, the transactional, focused and systematic approach of linked-in means it's a good place to get results.

It's truly come of age since it created discussion groups. These have been set up by professional bodies such as the Institute of Directors and the Chartered Institute of Marketing and gives the media savvy entrepreneur the opportunity to establish your reputation on topics directly relating to your core expertise.

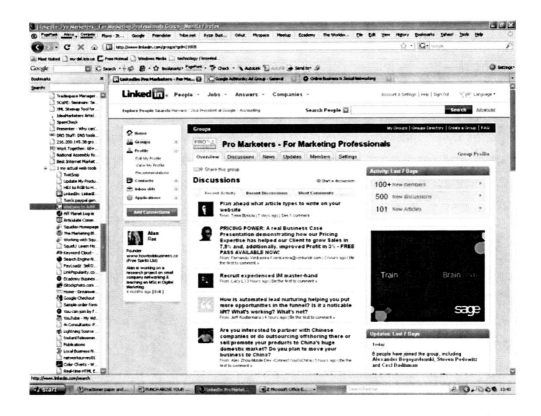

Some of the larger forums are quite powerful. Experience shows that it takes up to 1000 members of a forum before it takes on a life of its own. One good example is the Pro Marketing Forum which is now rapidly becoming a powerhouse of information with currently about 30 discussions being started off each day.

Twitter

Twitter is something that you need to know about – even if it doesn't suit your business at this point. Like many things in the online world it has quite suddenly gone through a transformation. From being something that was the private space of geeks and technical journalists to something that's becoming part of the daily toolkit of web-aware marketers.

It's permission marketing writ large. People decide to follow you if they think what you have to say is fun or useful. If you bore them – they'll abandon you.

Effectively it's microblogging. You have 140 characters to get your message across – better than a Google ad – but not much. Its benefit is you can include a link to something you want people to know about – a Blog post, an invitation to and event, a special offer.

Like everything else in the networking world being interesting and conversing rather than broadcasting is what will build your personal brand. That and being authentic. This is where the small business has a real advantage over the corporate. You can use your passion and belief in your product and your team to advantage.

The way to manage it is to use a tool like Hootsuite to automate your "business" posts. You can then dip in and out to chat with your colleagues, re-tweet things you thing will interest your followers and generally use it as a platform to inform and entertain. If you keep the proportion of promotional posts to around 15% it should be fine.

People claim that they are getting more business through twitter than other channels– if they are known subject experts. Twitter will help you build a following.

The other great thing is you can link RSS feeds to it via utilities like www.twitterfeed.com which effectively collects RSS feeds and sends to the link. There are other tools which are useful in supporting it – Tweetdeck to help you sort the conversations out and create lists, And Hootsuite to help you automate your posts.

It acts effectively as a connecting tool also – you can route blogs and other posts via twitter to end user destinations in Facebook, for example

So having reviewed what's available let's select the media you will use to tell your story. We've taken a long detour through the online area because the chances are that you either do this already or you avoid it. We think you should know what you're missing.

However the fact remains – you have 12.5 hours a week to do all your selling, networking and marketing. To make a decent fist of being online you are probably going to need at least an hour a day – and probably more some days.

You need to come up with a Blog post of 300-400 words every week and maintain a good presence on one main network and a couple of profiles on others. However if you use the tools cleverly it's surprising how much effect you can have.

If you are like most of the people surveyed the other tools you will use to promote yourself apart from face to face selling, one to ones and networking will be

- PR

- Workshops

- Email

Most of you avoid things like exhibitions, direct mail, telemarketing and postcards and leaflet drops and inserts.

But you have to get the optimum balance right between online and offline, marketing and networking and selling for your own particular business.

We think it would be a good time now for you to revisit what you plan to do in the light of what we've told you about the internet marketing tools.

And remember – this is all about finding your top 50 people.

If you have a local non scalable business you might do well enough with local networking and a modest web presence.

However if you want to promote your genius internationally – you may end up doing a lot on-line.

Bonus Section – online copywriting

The key thing with online copywriting is that you are writing for 2 audiences, the human one who needs to be guided towards a call to action and a robotic one who will allow the page to be found or the email to be let through the spam filter.

For Web pages the gatekeeper is Google. Will the page show up on the search engine when someone carries out a relevant search either organic or by paid search. Otherwise we are reliant on

> links from partner organisations or social media presences we've created

> Or traffic we drive towards the page using email.

The problem is that the needs of the two readers conflict.

"Free" and "Help" are two great words for motivating humans – but they are markers of Spam and may lead to your carefully crafted email being eaten alive before your potential customer ever sees it. Trying to navigate our way through this needs focus.

In conventional copywriting it's always a good idea to spend a lot of time on the headline – some authorities think you should spend up to half your time on it – or even more. It's even more important in these electronic environments. Because that may be all you have to carry your message in the case of email.

We'll have to tackle the two media separately but there are some principles of similarity that it's worth focusing on – we'll look at these next.

First some more psychology. This next section is distilled from Robert Cialdini's book Influence, Science and Practice[xvii] which I strongly recommend you read.

Cialdini argues that we are on automatic pilot most of the time. When we make decisions we make snapshot judgements. Our brains did not evolve to make rational decisions effectively. They evolved to get us out of trouble quickly. From a certain point of view, the human brain is a machine for creating a pattern quickly – for taking two and two and making five.

That's why it operates in short cuts. We only THINK about something in depth

> If we can

> If it matters

So the aim of copywriting is to present something in such a way that the decision to say yes goes by default.

In the web environment the tendency to act automatically on cues is exaggerated because people don't read – they scan. And they have got used to looking in specific places for information.

And to taking notice of material that stands out and is in certain specific places.

Can you think of some examples of this in practice?

A great resource for understanding how the web environment works is Jacob Nielsen's www.Useit.com site. It's full of good stuff such as how many people do you need to test a site (the answer is 15 but you should find and read the article to find out why

Nielsen says that people scan the page – not read it.

So he recommends you use

Highlighted Key-words

Meaningful (not clever) sub-headings

Bulleted Lists

One Idea per paragraph

Half the word count – English fortunately lets us do this

He argues that the web has trained us to want information quickly and efficiently – if we can't find it within 7 seconds we'll go elsewhere. So the message must be crystal clear and easily accessible.

Cialdini reinforces this by reminding us that what influences us are:

Contrast – we notice things that stand out

Reciprocation – which is why free offers work – if I do something for you then you should do something for me. The same principles apply in networking.

Surprise – like contrast – it gets noticed.

Consistency – which is why branding is so important

Social Proof – so testimonials or links from influential sites are important

Things to do with the customer feeling comfortable that they will have a good experience

Liking

Symmetry –   the golden mean

Association with good things

Authority – appearance, carriage, gaze, height. On line we have to rely on graphics, font, colour and links to authoritative sites.

Scarcity / Things for with limited availability / Things that are banned

Writing it out or saying it makes it true – so any form of interaction will strengthen the memory of what you have to offer

Our task is to deliver as many of these as are practical within a language and framework that will appeal to the persona of our target customer and within a space that will work on a smart phone.

Conventional Copywriters tell you to start with the Headline

If your headline doesn't sell your product you've wasted 90% of your money according to David Ogilvie.

In fact, a good headline will boost sales by 17% if used with the same body copy. It must

> Attract attention
>
> Communicate a strong benefit
>
> Answer the WIIFY (what's in it for you) factor
>
> Set the tone for the offer

Professional Copywriters advise.

> Don't use more than 17 words
>
> Use quotes – its more memorable and pulls 28% more
>
> Use upper and lower case
>
> Don't vary the type size
>
> Put the headline below the picture

This is all from the point of view of humans. Online you have to take into account your robot audience so you should use keywords for headlines and sub heads in order to attract a search engine audience

How much do you consciously do this now? What could you do to do a better job?

So – you need a headline and a call to action.

But in between we need to build on the narrative implied in the headline so as to address the reader's pain or desire for gain or knowledge. The costs of staying ignorant – of not being included in the know for instance.

The first paragraph has to really make the client sit up and take notice. If you get it right and the layout is good, the decision will be made by the end of the first paragraph. If you are writing for the web, try to seed the first sentence with a couple of relevant keywords.

You need to end with a strong call to action – come to the seminar, buy this report etc.

So try writing a headline, a first paragraph and a call to action for one of your products here.

So far we've been largely talking about the copy itself and the interplay with the customers. However there's a lot more to writing good web pages.

A great site needs to integrate

Design

How the operations work

Usability

The words

How its optimised to attract traffic

How its hosted

Design Layout is also critical. Good sites are easy to navigate. You may not have much control over that but you do have control over where you put your text on the page. All the research based on tracking eye movements of people reading web pages suggests that they scan the page in an F shape.

That means they look across the top, Then down the side and lastly across the middle from left to right. The headline should go at the top of the F which will be about 1/3 way down and 3 inches in and it should focus on pain or gain and then be amplified in the first paragraph. Here's the evidence, courtesy of Jakob Nielsen which points up where people actually look.

http://www.useit.com/alertbox/reading_pattern.html

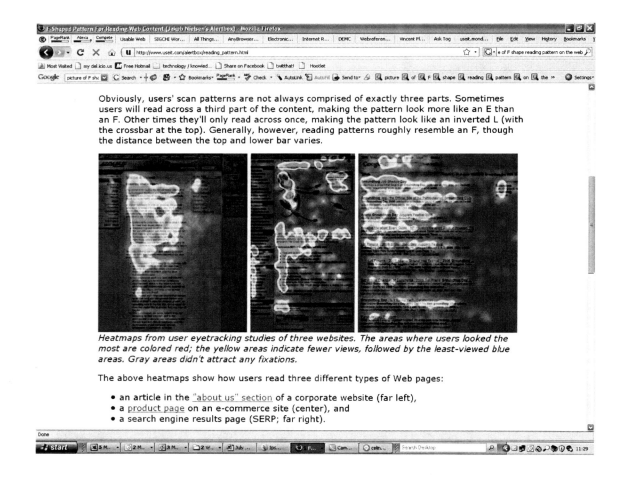

This is prime web property – don't waste it

Apart from positioning, Jakob Nielsen argues that web credibility is built by

High Quality Graphics

Good Writing

     Present tense,

     Short paragraphs

     Short colourful vital words

     Motivational

Social Proof

     Outbound Links that say what they are to our business partners

     Other relevant sources of information

     Available biographies of key players

     Availability of archive material

     Links to background information instead of long scrolling pages

He urges that you use normal internet conventions – underlined hyperlinks for example.

Above all DON'T BE TOO CLEVER

Outline what social proof you could deliver

Copywriting for Email

Email presents particular challenges for the novice copywriter. You still have to have the same punchy ness and appeal in the headline and opening paragraph but you also have to avoid getting tangled up with the spam filters and avoid having people complain.

Most email clients turn off graphics by default and there are several legal constraints that you need to be aware of.

    The headline must make clear it's a commercial offer

    People need to have the chance to unsubscribe

    You need to have your full company details in the footer.

The great words like free and discount will send your offering to the oubliette but there are traps for the unwary such as those innocent words "help" "discount" and "reminder" will have the spam filters sinking their fangs into your innocent email.

It's important that you work with a clean up to date list of people who have given you permission to contact them. Complaints will get you blacklisted as will sending emails to addresses that are defunct. So don't do it. Once you get your site blacklisted it can be really hard work getting it unstuck.

It's recommended not to make the email more than 600 pixels wide because we don't know what machine or browser it will appear in. It might be appearing in a blackberry or other PDA. An individual might have given you a personal email – hotmail, yahoo, Gmail etc and these don't like large graphics or links very much.

Even if it's being read on a desk machine, chances are its being read in a preview screen which may be narrowly set. Chances are also good that the graphics will be turned off by default and your recipient will not feel it worthwhile to turn it on unless he has a good reason. So use the Alt text tag to tell them what it is. But rely on the text to carry the message

To deal with the preview pane issue the advice is

> Ensure important content is at the side of the preview pane
>
> Have your logo top left to add credibility
>
> Try and get your call to action above the scroll

Here's how AOL do it to give you an idea of what you have to contend with.

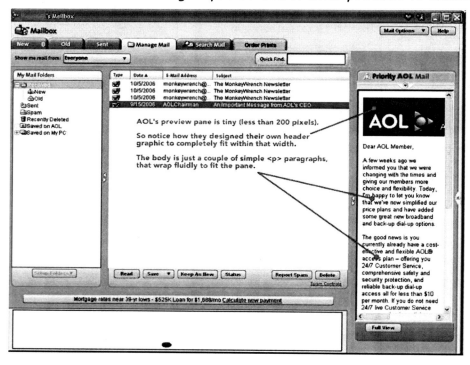

Image from MailChimp – an emailing service that's giving us some good results.

How effective is Email?

For most industries you can assume that a good list and a well crafted email will achieve a 20-30% opening rate.

Typical click through rates will be between 2.5% and 6% for most sectors. Hard bounce rates are between 2 and 8% with the rates for soft bounces being somewhat lower. Unsubscribes are typically 3 in 1000 and abuse complaints 1 in 1000

Here's a useful post campaign checklist from MailChimp

How many emails failed to be successfully delivered? If an abnormally high number of emails bounced, read through some email headers to find out why.

Did people click on the links I wanted them to click? If so, did they register or did I lose my sales somewhere in the website?

If people didn't click on what I wanted them to, how can I change my next campaign to improve my click rates?

How many people normally unsubscribe from each of my campaigns? Did this campaign result in more or less unsubscribes than usual? Do you know why people are unsubscribing? Have you setup an online survey link in your opt-out confirmation screen and email? Look through those results as well.

What was my open rate for this particular campaign, and how does this compare to my "normal" open rate? Did anything change? Why?

Is there any particular day/time that seems to work best for my campaigns?

Are people still opening and clicking now, or has activity pretty much died down?

How much money did this campaign cost me? Did/will it pay off?

Some thoughts on constructing offers

In the "Paradox of Choice", Barry Schwartz describes research that clearly demonstrates that too much choice is counterproductive.[xviii]

As we mentioned earlier our nervous systems evolved to make binary choices – stay or go – fight or flight – do or not do (there is no try).

We can (if we have to) get the scientific method out of the cupboard and make a rational choice – but we won't thank you for it. We'll put off the decision if you force us into rational mode – and if we do decide – then the buyer's remorse will be terrible. So don't make us think. That's why copywriters through the ages focus on getting us to stay with the gut and create something that feels familiar and innocently enticing if they want us to buy.

Schwartz quotes some evidence from a project carried out on people buying Sony and Aiwa sound systems. It turns out that if you make

I good offer – 66% of the sample bought

2 alternative good offers - 53% bought

1 good and 1 unattractive offer - 73% bought

So provide an offer and a benchmark. This could be a highly priced all inclusive offer as well as the one you actually want them to buy.

If you provide someone with an all inclusive bundle and then offer them a reduction for each item they take out, you'll do better than if you offer a base price + supplementary prices for add-ins. Because psychologically the pain of giving something up is greater than the gain of adding something to a basic specification

He concludes that people want to have choices made easy for them.

Complexity forces them to trade off which makes them put off deciding.

Conflict reduces mental well-being and so reduces decisiveness.

Schwartz also describes some interesting findings about HOW people choose. They'll forgo an uncertain large gain in favour of a certain small gain and conversely they'll risk a complete disaster that's not certain to avoid a small reverse that will certainly happen.

One other factor that's counter intuitive is that people also buy to avoid post purchase regret. Some people – Schwartz calls them Maximisers – spend a long time to make sure that they get the best possible available deal. Others, labelled Satisficers, are more relaxed.

If you believe that you are writing for Maximisers then you will need to try and make the offer appear the obvious, safe and logical choice. All the research points to the view that decisions taken by gut feeling lead to less buyer's remorse than decisions taken with a great degree of analytic input.

So if you are dealing with people who need evidence, present it so that the case is unanswerable. And bear in mind how they'll react if the don't get what they think you offered them.

How might you present the evidence to be most convincing?

Part 2 Practical – Developing your Plan

We've gone through a lot of theory about networks, psychology, sales processes and how people respond to images and copy. We've reviewed some of the major social media tools at our disposal and thought a little about how they might work together. We've also looked at what your fellow business owners do based on our research projects and how different types of business need different approaches.

And we've identified that it's important to build a reputation for being knowledgeable, competent and easy to work with.

So now it's time to decide what our story is, and how much effort we want to put into each marketing activity. While having at the back of our minds how we are going to identify those key 50 people we want to influence.

Let's start with the story. As we've just been reviewing writing decent copy is a key skill of the small business owner.

It's important when writing copy to think of who you're addressing – and write directly to them taking into account the ideas about how they are likely to think and feel.

How you express yourself will depend on the medium. So when writing press releases they need to be kept short and factual with the key messages up front.

If you are writing an email it needs to be short and punchy.

If you are writing a direct mail piece it can be much longer – still use powerful headlines and benefits with the key messages at the beginning and end but salted throughout with triggers.

Just remember Cialdini and the key behaviour influencers

Authority, Social Proof (hence the value of testimonials) Contrast, Consistency, Reciprocation (hence the power of the free gift) the seductiveness of the forbidden, time limits, scarcity etc.

Good copywriting makes use of all of these while being succinct, punchy, colourful and easy to read.

PR is the most under-rated tool in the Small Business armoury. If you have a good story to tell, the local or trade press are often happy to use it. It builds brand like nothing else and can bring in orders from across the globe.

As we've discussed, on-line activities parallel off-line. So the on line equivalent of PR is blogging. If you write something regular in a place where it is picked up by the search engines with your name and key words attached it is astonishing how quickly it gets picked up.

The front page of Ecademy is a good place. It has an Alexa ranking of around 6000 currently and anything appearing there gets Googled pretty quickly. For a small company this is an easy cheap and quick way to boost traffic to your site.

Just remember with all of these activities that you are aiming to produce a continuing flow of warm leads – probably through your site. So a good way of attracting visits and collecting email addresses is to offer free downloads through your site – giving information that's of value away in exchange for permission to contact with further offers of what you wish to sell.

So let's work on your story

Your story is how you are going to make an initial emotional contact with your customer. Now try this exercise. If you focus on your needs and values and those of the customers you can see if any narrative immediately drops out of the analysis.

What is our Story?

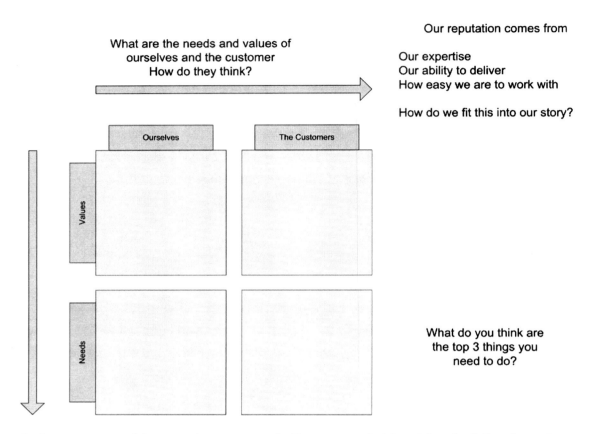

So have a go at this now. As an example I once used this with a building firm. It turned out that both they and their customers wanted a good job done on time with out too much commercial aggravation

So their story evolved from the idea of traditional values in the modern world. This for them was quite powerful.

So what's your story – in outline from your point of view.

So lets think some more about the customer. So now you're ready to identify what their pain might be. What is the problem that your customer can't fix himself?

What is the damage that it's doing to his organisation?

What will the world look like to him with your service in place to him?

Write your story out again here in the detail you need. You want to be clear about what you do – how it addresses the customer's pain – how you relate to their needs and values and what the future will be like with your solution embedded in it.

So now you need to de-construct your story into some key chunks to use in different situations. Take a few minutes to carry out these tasks

HEADLINE – generally you should spend about 40% of the time getting this right. On-line it should include the keywords that people use to find you.

First Paragraph – This is what connects you emotionally with the client. How does what you do help them realise their hopes – or deal with their fears.

Keywords – the words and phrases that you want to own in the customer's mind – and online in Google's too. At this stage I want you to just brainstorm these. We'll do some analysis in a moment.

Homing in on your keywords

Having brainstormed them – lets think about how we can systematically home in on the ones that really work.

Google ad-words is the place to start. The first thing you should do is sign up for an account. Google will prefer you to sign up with an ID based on a Gmail address. I would suggest you do that as you can use it as an open ID for tools like Twitterfeed etc and this will save you a lot of time later on.

Once you've created an account, Google will ask you for a credit card number. You can be relaxed about this because it won't take any money from you until you activate the programme. Now find the keyword tool. The best way to do this is to go to the tools menu and select keyword tool from the menu

This will allow you to put some of your brainstormed keywords into the box to generate variants and estimate likely traffic.

Then you can select the phrases that you want to test – don't forget that keyword phrases are quite often up to 4 words long.

This will help you be more specific in developing your messages.

So here's an example of what you get. I've used "psychological profiling for leadership" as an example from my BrainMap promotional activities. What we're looking for are phrases that have a reasonable volume but a modest amount of

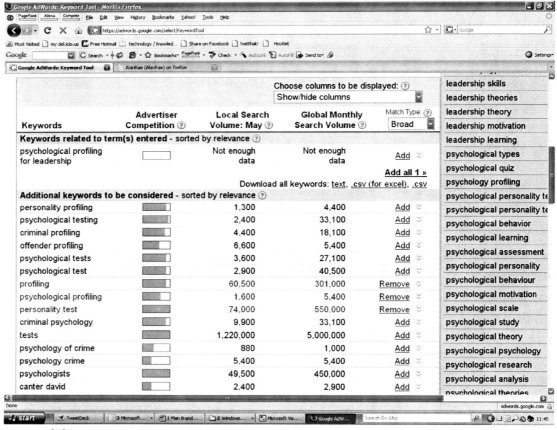

competition.

On the face of it "psychological analysis" looks like a reasonable bet as it has 6600 searches per month and is only 50% of the way up the competitive scale. "Psychological profiling" has much less competition but only a quarter of the traffic. While "personality test" has massive traffic (550,000 per month) - but maximum competition. It's also not good because it's quite non specific and will likely have a high cost per click.

So what it tells us is how much traffic, how much the cost per click and what he likely position for these key words is likely to be – as here

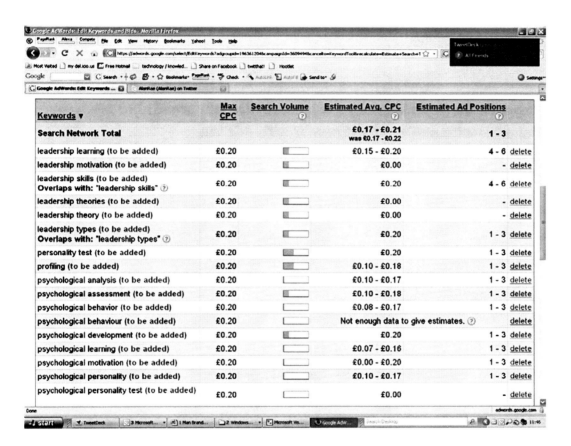

Now there are plenty of people who say that this gives you the information you need. Personally I think you need to run a test campaign as well. It can be quite inexpensive – if you cap it at £3 a day that's £100 a month or if you cap it at £5 a day, that's £500 in 3 months. What it will give you is the chance to test these words in anger against an advert.

You tell Google that every time someone searches for this word you want to bet – say 20P. This means that you are prepared to pay 20p to have the ad shown –

Google will work out how far up the page it goes according to the competition. If someone clicks on the ad you know that

There's some traffic for that word

Your ad is working.

So staying with the Brain Map example, phrases like left brain, right brain and brain map work quite well and I get results with Ads like

Left Brain Right Brain

The BrainMap shows how people think

So you can communicate better

www.howtodobusiness.com

This has produced a lot of inexpensive clicks over the years.

You can use the results to test which keywords produce the best results by analysing how they perform in terms of click conversions and how well they end up in actual sales.

Once you know which the best keywords are, you can put them as the anchor text (this is the text that appears on the underlined part of the link) on links back to your site from profiles you create in social media and in headlines, first paragraphs and page title tags on your site.

You can use them to tag Blog articles, you-tube videos, diagrams and photographs and any other on line assets that you have in social media sites so that they will associate your web pages with these phrases.

Now I'd like you to write a Google Ad to convey your offer so that you can practice refining your copywriting skills. Google ads consist of a headline of 25 characters, 2 lines of 35 characters and a specific landing page URL

Headline – 25 characters

Sentence 1 – 35 chars

Sentence 2 – 35 chars

And I'd also like you to try your hand at expressing your story as a 140 character tweet. These exercises are really powerful for getting you to sharpen up how you express yourself.

Now I'd like you to write a twitter biography – you have 71 characters only. Mine is "Turning knowledge into wisdom since 1981. Research / Structure / Present / Set to Music"

Having got the story and the keywords for tagging sorted out you need to think about how many leads you actually need to generate

This – will depend on

How much money you want

How big the unit of sale is

How much your unit cost is?

How high your overheads are

How complicated you sales cycle is.

The diagram makes clear that until your revenue is equal to your variable costs + fixed costs you don't have a business.

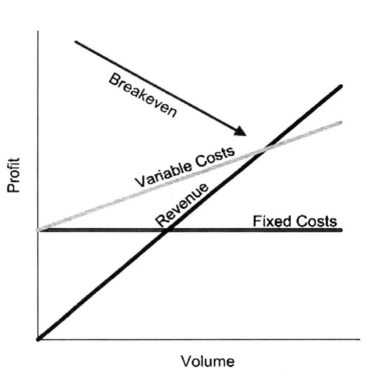

But the shape of these graphs will depend on whether you are selling an online plant for £30 – or a nuclear power plant for £30 million.

Each sale you make will deliver you a unit of contribution. You need to know how many units you need to make per month to pay the wages and deliver the profit that you want.

And then you need to know how much activity you need to make that sale. – And what the steps of the sales process are. So if your activity depends on face to face selling – the pattern will be different from activity that depends on selling products through a web site.

You need to have some awareness of how many touches the client on average has to have with you or your company before they actually buy anything.

The position is made more complicated if you have to sell services via a web site in which case you may need to organise a download of some kind of proof of competence – this might be a free tool – like a marketing planner or 10 things you should know about recruiting an accountant / plumber / copywriter.

I can't give you a formula that fits all circumstances – but here are two examples. Your have to work out what your own pipeline process looks like and how much activity you need from each source to make it work reliably.

Anyway – let's make a start

How much money do you want to make per month	A	£
How much overhead per month do you have to cover	B	£
How much contribution do you make per sale	C That's Sale price – costs of goods -costs of selling	£
So how many sales do you need to make per month	D = A+B/C	4?
What's your ratio of closable sales to sales	3:1?	12?
How many face to face meetings per close	2:1?	24?
How many telephone conversations per face to face meeting	3:1?	72?
How many downloads per telephone conversation	2:1?	144?
How many site visits per download	3:1?	432?
How Many Impressions per site visit	50:1?	20K+?
So how many sales do you need to make per month	D = A+B/C	2000
Visit order form	5:1?	10000?
Get to product page	2:1?	20000?
Landing Page to Product Page	5:1?	100k?
Impressions per site visit	50:1?	5M?

I've given you 2 routes here – 1 for services and 1 for online sales of not too expensive products. The actual route may vary – when I used to sell CAD systems for a living it was something like

enquiries / visit
visit / proposal
Proposal / demonstration
Demonstration / Sale

The theory being that you closed on the demonstration– although life was rarely that straight forward. I suggest you start by filling in the table above as best you can – and then do the real thing by constructing your own table below.

Don't worry if it seems hard – that's because it IS hard.

How much money do you want to make per month	A	£
How much overhead per month do you have to cover	B	£
How much contribution do you make per sale	C That's Sale price – costs of goods -costs of selling	£
Sales process stage 4		
Sales process stage 3		
Sales process stage 2		
Sales process stage 1		
Marketing process stage 4		
Marketing process stage 3		
Marketing process stage 2		
Marketing process stage 1		

Strategy

So now we need to work out what your strategy should be – how are you actually going to achieve the leads and sales you need? As we mentioned above you need to be thinking about how the leads are going to come to you.

> Are you selling a service where you have to carry out a lot of face to face activity – because actually they want to see you?

> Are you carrying out a service where people will refer you to people you may never meet based on your reputation.

> Are you selling products from a web site where you never need to meet people at all?

People buy when their need to solve a problem or their desire to own something pushes them forward and your solution looks like the best bet when an often random balance of perceived quality weighed against the costs and risks of doing business tips in your favour.

The costs side of the balance are a subtle combination of your actual price, the perceived risks of doing business with you and your reputation which again is a subtle balance of likeability, ease of doing business and professionalism.

All of these balance eventually come together into a brand. The importance of the brand will vary according to what you're selling. But there's no doubt that good professional graphics and photography and easy to read, well laid out text make a big difference.

Your strategy is going to be framed by

How you get noticed by your target audience – Visibility

How they perceive your value / risk + costs - Credibility

How you can deliver enough business in a financially sound manner – Profitability.

This depends what you're selling. The challenges of selling research and insights are different from those if you're selling low allergy face products.

As a small business, you need to know where you sit on these continuums that we covered in the theoretical part. What the diagram actually shows is the balances between online and offline, scalable and non scalable and local vs. global businesses. The types of business that our research shows favour these particular approaches are shown in the boxes at each end of the arrows.

So try and pinpoint yourself on these criteria and identify which type of business you are in the diagram

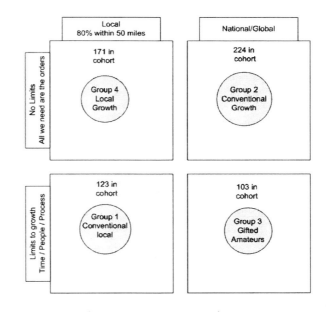

on the next page. Look at where you sit on those continuums. The categories in the boxes are the types of company that reported themselves at that end of the scale during our research.

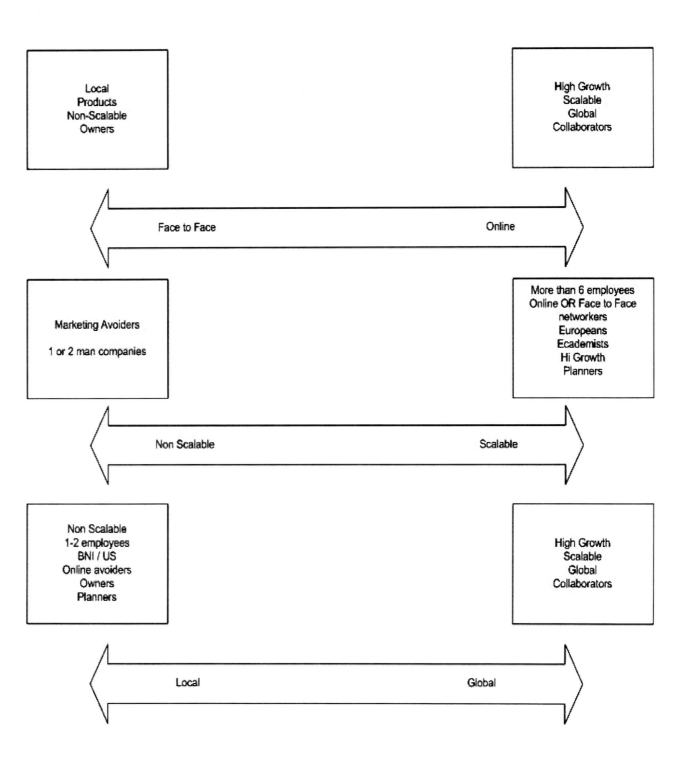

I think you will need some kind of a web presence whatever you're selling because people expect it. Even if you are planning a purely face to face campaign, people will want to go Google you ahead of meeting you – or afterwards. So it's important that you have something there that gives a good impression of who you are and what you do. You may also need to drive traffic to the site more proactively if that's what your business model needs.

To help you think about it – have a look at this diagram from our Punch above Your Weight Programme

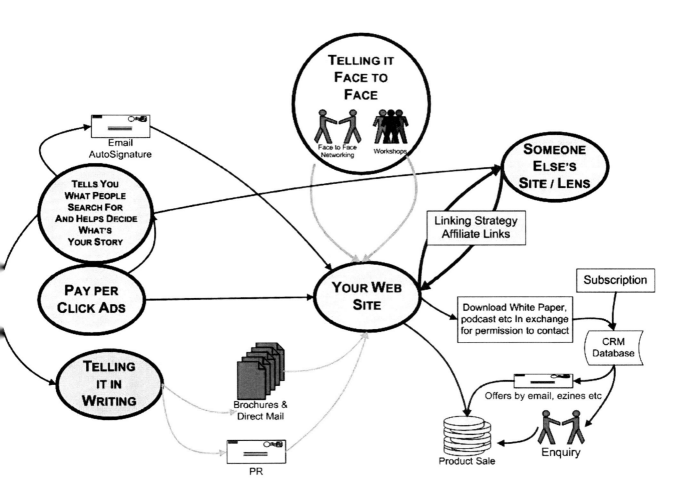

.What it's telling us is that you can drive traffic to a site by

Meeting people face to face – networking, exhibitions, workshops

From Adwords or Organic Search

From Links on someone else's site

From written materials – PR, Postcards, Brochures, fliers, white papers,

Emails, Direct Mail pieces that send the individual to look on line

So let's review the strategic issues and then focus in on the detail of what techniques will suit you and how exactly you're going to make use of them.

The point is – you have to generate a certain number of enquiries – if its just you and you only need 1 consultancy project per 6 months, your strategy is very different from one in which you need 1 sale a week – or as in our plants business 250 – 300 sales a week.

Based on our research into how people actually promote themselves, we've identified that its companies that want to operate on a global stage that carry out more online activity – using primarily linked-in and twitter, online social networks and blogs.

The following table sets out what types of business use which media'

	Local	Global/National
Scalable	**One to One Selling** **Networking** Blogs PR Workshops Online Advertising	**One to One Selling** **Networking** Workshops Online Advertising PR Blogs Newsletters Email Shots *Example - plants4presents Sells plants online*
Non Scalable	**One to One Selling** **Networking** Workshops Online Advertising *Example Fletching Glasshouses Organic Veg*	**One to One Selling** **Networking** Online Advertising Email shots Print Advertising PR *Example HowtodoBusiness - research and training*

Apart from the obvious conclusion that National businesses use a wider range of tools and that everyone uses one to one selling, networking and online advertising, what tools do you think you should be using the most?

You need a core body of purposeful, targeted activity – face to face selling and networking with a supportive group of 20-40 people that you're going to develop ultimately into business partners. You'll also spend time on deliberate connections via linked-in, driving traffic to the site through Adwords and links.

But in the social media life is random – you may make a connection with ANYONE in environments like Ecademy and Twitter, via your Blog and whatever online profiles you build. If you have the kind of business that requires that sort of reach – national or global – then it makes sense to embed your core activity of purposeful activity in a cyber sphere of randomness.

As long as you are absolutely clear about what you're doing, the more people who know you, the more likely the people you would never have normally met will find you.

Thomas Power – Chairman of Ecademy – believes that finding the 50 people in the world who are really relevant to your business may take up to 1000 connections each before they become apparent.

Within the context of setting up a basic marketing plan, the key principles you need to be aware of are

Understanding how influence works and creating some basic pieces of collateral to allow you to fulfil the principles of "Givers Gain"

Understanding what simple mechanisms exist to identify the ways your target audience describes your offers and how to use these words as tags in various social media as appropriate

Understanding the basic principles of copywriting particularly in an online environment

Knowing how to create and disseminate pieces of online collateral in an integrated way.

Understanding how online activity is channelled towards a result in the online environment. The strategy will be different depending on whether the end result is

A sale

A downloaded piece of collateral

Contact by phone or email

A conversation

Building an online Reputation

Reputation is based on proofs of competence – or failing that testimonials and a prompt response.

Online and Offline networking need to be based on respect and listening rather than moving immediately into Spam Mode

You need to identify your key group to network with and be clear about what you do and what you want to be recommended for.

So write down here how you are going to deliver some of these key criteria. After clarity of story which we've already discussed the other things you need to present – both online and offline are

Reciprocity – what are you going to do for them first? – An introduction, a free object of value?

Social Proof - testimonials - good position in other networks - how might you build this?

Consistency so you seem solid and have a reputation for following up. How will this be conveyed?

Building a collateral library.

We've talked a lot about how to be clear about what you do but you need to be systematic about developing the evidence you need to prove that you mean what you say.

Creating documents that explain what you're about and can act as a guide to prospective customers without impacting your ability to sell to them is useful.

You should consider creating – or having created –

a couple of 2-3 page articles

an 8-12 page document which covers the basics of how to use your service written to create informed customers

A 60-80 page e-book – about the size of this document.

You can use these in various ways to support your credibility.

You can have free-downloads from you site – which you can promote using Adwords to test what keywords your target audience actually responds to. You can set up systems (mail-chimp is one, constant contacts is another) which will allow people access to this material in exchange for permission to contact them.

You can sell the e-book through the site OR you can use it as a give-away for workshop attendees OR you can chop it up into 500 word gobbets and create a serialised Blog – OR you can chop it up into 140 character tweets and tell your story to your followers.

All of these will support your networking and other marketing activities – provide the material you need for effective "Givers Gain" and provide that Solid online presence of quality material that you want people to find when they Google you.

Other things you might consider are creating podcasts or videos using you-tube or photos and tag these with your keywords. You can even use little tools called "widgets" which can contain blogs or links to FaceBook fan pages and leave these scattered about on blog pages, internet profiles or other internet environments that you may control.

Putting this together is a time consuming project – but it's worth it.

So let me ask you to spend a little time planning this and to come up with the titles of the materials you want create

Title and outline content of first 2 page document

Title and outline content of second 2 page document

Title and overall content of 12 page document

Title and overall content of 60 page document

This material needs to be interesting, informative, well written and laid out and not salesy. It's important as collateral in the online world because it gives you ways of interacting with potential new clients.

You can use this to engage with them and then on the strength of your writing get them to subscribe to your Blog or your newsletter. My friend Fraser Hay always describes things like this as free items of value.

Their importance is that they give you ways of rewarding people as you build the relationships with them that will ultimately lead to business.

For instance if they connect with you on Ecademy you can automate it so that they are offered a free item. If they complete a research survey. If they sign up for your newsletter. If they sign up to come to a workshop. These all add value from you to them. If you are running a professional services business these are all powerful additions to your marketing mix.

Building your position as an expert

Having identified your niche and what you want to offer - you should aim to position yourself as THE EXPERT in your chosen field.

And the tools that you have to deploy this information are

Social media including networking sites, blogs, twitter and you-tube

Conventional PR

Workshops

Follow up Email Shots

Let's try and sequence this a little bit according to the growth of your relationship with the potential customer.

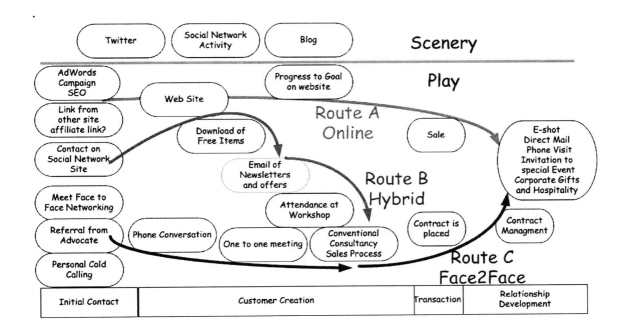

The goal is to develop a profitable continuing partner relationship. The Sale or transaction is simply a step on the way. You can't build a business through a series of one off sales because eventually the costs of customer acquisition will kill you.

So we've divided this into a series of stages from initial contact via relationship building through a transaction to the development of a long term relationship. We've identified some of processes that are available for different types of business model. Route A in Blue is a pure online scenario. Route C in Green is a pure face to face model suitable for business services while Route B in orange is a hybrid whereby you are using the tools of web 2.0 and the internet to feed potential customers ultimately into route C but with much of the prospecting effort automated.

As you can see I've divided the activities into Scenery and Play. The Play can happen without the scenery – but it's better if the Scenery is there.

135

I include activity in twitter, blogs and social networks as scenery because for most of us it's about helping people find us and making sure that there's good current evidence that we're good at what we do and that other people respect us. That's not to say they can't be used directly to create sales via route A – but since most businesses surveyed are in personal or business services we've focused on the routes shown.

So let's think about which tools you might use in your business – take the time to think through the options and pick one or two from each list.

What's the best face to face networking group for you? BNI, Ecademy, Professional Organisation, Lunch meetings, Chamber of commerce etc.

What tools will drive traffic to your site Google Ad-words, Social Media, You-tube, Links, Articles, Affiliates, other on line advertising and Email. Podcasts

What written tools will you use? Postcards, Brochures, PR, Email, Web Pages, E-books, White papers, Direct Mail

What other Face to Face tools will you use?

One to one meetings, structured Selling, workshops and exhibitions. Hospitality and corporate gifts.

How are you going to build your online presence?

The most important thing is how you are going to fit it all in.

The good news is that you don't need to write everything out from scratch. Almost all social media these days is connected together. The fundamental insight is that you need a couple of source media where you create – Ecademy, a WordPress Blog for example (and don't forget You-Tube here).

You need a carrier medium which everything feeds into and which is picked up elsewhere – (Twitter seems to be starting to fulfil this role) and various "sink" media where your ideas end up and where you can connect to other people. Linked-in and Facebook are the Prime examples of this in practical terms as I write this.

You will also want to use these tools to drive traffic to your site via organic search. If the pieces are tagged with your best key words which can be found by carrying out some structured research with Google ad-words then you can get a second bite at the cherry – particularly if you build it into your autosignature as anchor text in places like Ecademy. It all hangs together like this.

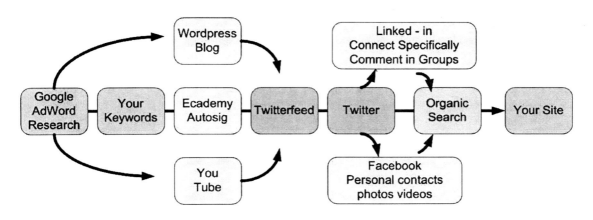

Let's work through how these steps work operate.

We covered how you can test your keywords via use of Google Adwords. The next stage is to understand how to use these words to tag pieces of online collateral such as Blog posts, Ecademy posts or you tube videos.

When a Blog is created, in WordPress you can put it into a category. If you use your keywords as categories – e.g. barriers to business growth, or small business marketing, then over time that phrase will become identified with your site and will start to climb the organic search rankings.

In the same way you-tube videos can be tagged with key-words. It is worth knowing that insight part of you-tube will give you valuable demographic information by age and gender of who's looking at your material.

Twitter is an effective medium for picking up and disseminating the materials that you create.

You can send information to it via tools like Twitterfeed and tweet-later and have your twitter entries picked up in aggregation tools such as Facebook and friend feed while a WordPress Blog can be piped directly to your linked-in, Facebook and Ecademy profiles and into any web space that you happen to own via a blidget.

This does mean that you can start to write things once and then recycle them to create a much larger web profile.

Twitter

Let's look at twitter-feed. It requires you to set up an account using an open ID. Various log-ins will give you this including your WordPress ID or your Google Mail ID. This is anyway quite a useful one to have as a spare online email address so I recommend using that – as mentioned in the section on Adwords research.

Twitter feed allows you to set up posts from your sources and feed them to twitter account. It looks like this. The feeds are listed here.

WordPress blogs can be fed directly through using the format http://blog.howtodobusiness.com/feed.

You can also feed output from all Ecademy areas – market places, blogs, even clubs. The management at Ecademy have made the site twitter friendly. This means that anything you or anyone else posts can be tweeted at the touch of a button.

This is a really powerful tool if you want to be known as an expert in your chosen field. While we can use Twitterfeed to automatically send to twitter and posts we ORIGINATE ourselves, we may not wish to automate sending of all comments.

However if we are commenting on a Blog post that expresses our knowledge we can contribute it into the twitter stream.

As we've said before, the same laws apply in online networking as in offline. We build a reputation over time by being knowledgeable, doing what we say, being courteous and easy to work with.

To build trust on line, the audience want to know that there's a real person behind the post – not a spambot. So you need to be seen to be interactive in a constructive way – consistently.

So while it's ok to do a certain amount of trumpet blowing, no more than 10-15% of the posts should be about that. The rest should be either informative or conversational.

The way I deal with this is to use 2 main tools to manage my twittering.

One is Hootsuite, the other is Tweetdeck. Like most Twitter applications you can log into them with your twitter ID and they merely ask for you to confirm permission

Hootsuite allows you to stack up some future tweets. This means that you can build in your one or two "salesy" tweets per day at the beginning of the week and then forget about them. Hootsuite allows you to specify when you want it to go out – so randomise it a bit throughout the day.

That leaves you free to draw peoples attention to stuff that they might find interesting or to chat with people you know that have interesting on topic things to say as the opportunity crops up – the easiest way after all to appear real is to BE real.

So this is what it looks like. As you can see I have a list of tweets loaded up.

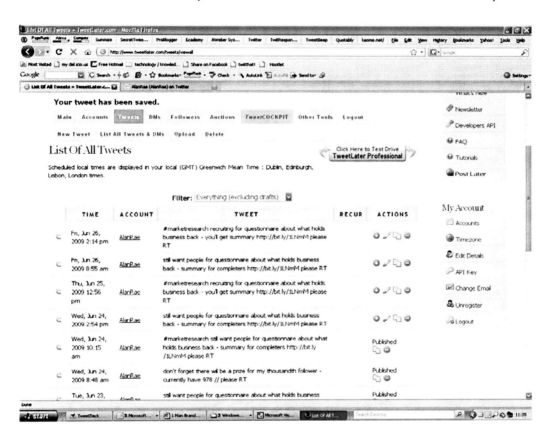

At the time of this screen grab I was pushing my newsletter and a survey that I was carrying out. Later today I can load up some references to workshops I want to promote and some free downloads.

The trick is to integrate it into the overall marketing mix – not treat it as something different.

Tweet deck is what makes it possible to manage what's going on. It's a client – there are others like seesmic and waterfall but I've got used to Tweetdeck – it looks like this. As you can see the left hand column tracks everything that anyone I follow says. The next 3 columns (which are user definable (up to 10 columns) let me track mentions, direct messages and replies

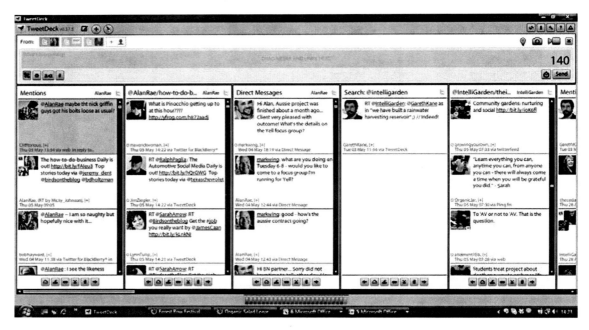

You can define other columns to track specific individuals or topics using what's called a hashtag.

#followfriday is another hashtag (sometimes shortened to #ff) that's worth knowing about as it does demonstrate very clearly our basic view that the online world reflects the offline reality.

#followfriday is a venerable twitter tradition that goes back at least as far as January 2010 - it's new and it feels like it's always been there. Every Friday it gives you the opportunity to recommend someone you think adds value to your life. So you can plug what they want plugged and say something nice about them all at the same time. It's of value because it helps to build trust. As we said earlier our research shows that the 3 key things that build trust are

- being clear about what you do
- getting back to people quickly
- following the principles of givers gain

Like lots of us I'm pretty poor at the first two - but it's easy to spend 10 minutes on a Friday morning giving a real time lift to people you value. So I think it's time well spent

I think that's about as much as I want to say about twitter within the context of this book except to mention www.hootsuite.com which allows you to tweet web pages that you're reading.

So here's some homework

Think of 3 things you want to tweet. Formula is headline and link – don't worry if the links too long – all the utilities will shorten it for you

Tweet 1

Tweet 2

Tweet 3

Now think of 3 people you want to recommend via a #followfriday. – Formula is #followfriday @alanrae because he really understands marketing ;)

First Contact

Second Contact

Third Contact

Finally – what hashtag would you choose for your own niche?

Facebook

Since the last edition of this book, Facebook has become considerably more important with a significant amount of traffic for online retail originating from within FaceBook.

You should at least consider creating a fan page and inviting your contacts to like it. You can hook it up to your blog and post videos, photos and encourage your friends and customers to use it as a tool to contact you.

Here's a picture of the fan page for www.theintelligentgarden.com

The page essentially consists of posts from the intelligent Garden blog, comments, and video and photo libraries.

At the time of writing it has over 200 fans and gets about 60 views a day.

Linked-in should almost certainly be a key part of your strategy if you are involved in the business to business world.

Our research shows clearly that it's the online networking environment of choice with over 40% of individuals with national or global businesses reporting that they used it regularly or depended on it.

It's the one area of online networking where there are plenty of corporate players and where you can only add someone to your network if you already have a connection – otherwise you have to be introduced.

You can add people if you already have their email address, if they are previous customers or people you've worked with or if you are members of the same group. Otherwise you have to be introduced to them by asking someone you know who knows them to pass you along. Linked-in will map the first 3 layers of connection. If you want to be introduced, the process looks like this.

Here's the profile of someone I worked with on a project a couple of years back. As you can see – he is in the third degree of separation from me. To connect with him I need to be referred my connection and then via one of his connections who's connected to one of mine.

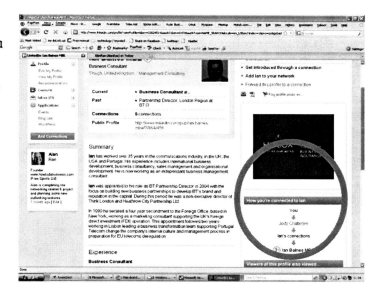

Fortunately because I already know Ian and have worked with him I can connect directly by mentioning the work position I held when we collaborated.

What has completely changed the game with Linked-in is that the have created groups – or special interest areas where people can pose or answer questions – here are some that I belong to.

Not only can I hold conversations with them and so spread knowledge of my professional expertise but I can also connect with other group members directly.

This makes building a structured rather than a random network comparatively easy. Although you have to be careful what you do with it.

However because the level of trust in linked in is by definition quite high (if you didn't have some kind of PROFESSIONAL connection with them you wouldn't be connected) then the quality of interaction will be comparatively high.

If you want to pose a question you can do so openly in a group or you can email up to 200 members of your own network. This means that you have SPECIFICALLY chosen them to receive the message. And the response rates will be higher. It's very good for getting responses to questionnaires or to get professional help. But as always it's advisable to be known as a contributor first.

The process of building and maintaining trust should always be at the front of your mind in on-line or off-line networking and this is no exception. Any spamming or MLM marketing in linked-in would get pretty short shrift.

A final quote from Thomas Power (based on his experiences with Ecademy. It takes 1 year to get noticed, 1 year to get liked and 1 year to get followed. On Linked- in its probably shorter because they already know you – but don't try and run before you can walk.

So – homework for Linked-in

Create your profile

Link your Blog to it – there's a widget if you work in WordPress

Invite your top 100 business connections to join you.

Join professional groupings that are natural for you to join

Start taking part in some of the discussions there

Look through your connections to see who you should be getting linked to and ask for introductions.

Start posing questions, and asking for and giving help.

This is one for the long haul

There is an overlap between connections on Ecademy, Linked-in and Facebook but you can use Ecademy and Facebook for the random side of building your network and linked-in for the purposeful side to supplement the activities of your home networking group.

You need to hold in your mind the idea that there are layers to your activity.

A close knit home support group for referrals and mutual support. In Dunbar number terms - backed up by our own research – this is likely to be between 20 and 40

A larger professional network maintained via linked-in. This is likely to contain around 150 people that you know well surrounded by a larger group of business acquaintances.

A much larger, more random network reached and managed via Ecademy, Facebook and Twitter. The core acquaintance group may be around a thousand or so with probably many more people who you really don't know but who have "connected" at some point. Of course, if your business is purely local you may not need this. However it's interesting how media like Twitter are starting to be important in keeping networkers in contact in our local town of Lewes.

Your way of interacting with it is by the production and exchange of useful information. On topic, Entertaining, compelling and motivating with a call to action. You create this in your Blog or on Ecademy or You-tube and disseminate it via the electronic media at your disposal or via face to face meetings and workshops.

You use this activity to drive traffic back to your site where further interaction and transactions can occur.

And you follow up the leads you generate in person. Face to face, by phone, by video conference. Your task now is to work out the right balance of online and offline activity that suits your business and will bring you the returns that you want.

Other tools you should consider

Before we go to the final summary plan section here's a quick review of some other tools you might consider.

Slideshare

If your business involves presenting knowledge in any kind of structured way you should think about putting PowerPoint presentations on www.slideshare.net

Knowledge products – for sale or for free – are a key part of the consultants or academic's stock in trade. Generally speaking we're all engaged in producing talks, slide sets and PDFs as a matter of course. The more adventurous of us may even created videos.

But whatever you produce needs to go somewhere where it will firstly be seen and secondly will give you some SEO benefit back to your own home base. There are several articles sites like articlebase, ezine articles and article dashboard but one location that gives you a real SEO benefit is Slideshare.

This lets you post slide sets as slides, PDFs etc. It also allows you to embed you-tube videos in the slide deck and to be notified of people who express an interest in contacting you. And it lets you embed your slides onto your linked-in profile. Consequently I rate this quite highly as a self publicity tool.

It looks like this.

YouTube

YouTube – alternatives Viddler or Vimeo - let you create small video clips of yourself in action as a musician, lecturer or facilitator. You can use a simple hand held digital VCR. Put it on a tripod and make sure you have decent lighting.

If you have that you can do quite a lot before having to use professional kit. I created some quite effective case studies for **www.growingjobs.org** like this in which horticulturalists told their own stories about some innovative approaches they'd taken to workforce development. There are a couple of examples on **www.theintelligentgarden.com**   plus of course the music videos on **www.heavenlyblues.com**

Of course it's all in the editing. If you need a professionally produced show reel – that's what you should pay for.

However to illustrate products in blogs or to produce case studies of people telling your story in their own words then a quick video of a couple of minutes embedded into an html page will work wonders. Here's a tip – it's often better to rehearse the shot a couple of times than to edit it afterwards. My experience is that the customers or people you interview need no rehearsing – it's the interviewer who needs to practice.

If you would rather just have some slides with a voice over you can create those using a tool called Camtasia.

I've used it extensively to produce Flash movies from PowerPoint slides. You can create these either just as slides or with a small "talking head" in the corner. It's also got the ability to do screen captures and to insert quizzes and tests so it can be used extensively for online training.

If you have enough clips you might consider creating a YouTube channel.

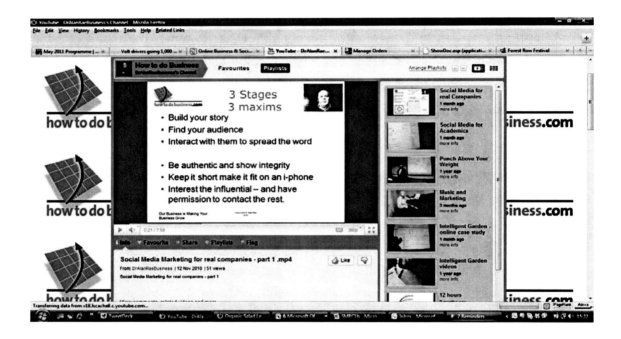

Mine looks like this. You can find it at www.youtube.com/dralanraebusiness

Books

If you have any published books, or even if you've created some of your own, you might consider setting up an author page on Amazon. As long as you have even a chapter in a book that's published there you can set up your own page. Many consultants and academics are writers so as long as you have an ISBN number for the works in question you can be a publisher. You can have your own author's page, your own bookstore and even if you just list some books you think people would benefit from reading – that in itself will have a SEO value in producing links back to your site.

This has quite powerful SEO effects. Here's an example of what one looks like.

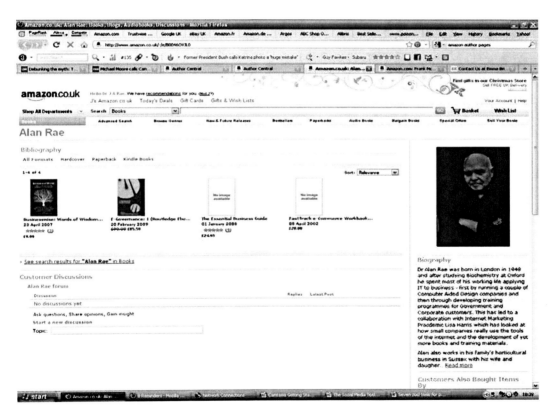

If you want to create paperback books of your own, like this one then check out www.completelynovel.com. I used their services to create this book

Paper.Li

The final tool you might like to check out is www.paper.li.

This is a really interesting tool which effectively creates a daily newspaper from the links embedded in a twitter stream. This can be created either from a defined list or from a topic using a hashtag such as #organicgardening

The wrong way to use this tool is whack everyone you follow into one big undifferentiated paper and tweet it every day. This will turn your followers off in droves and has resulted in anti Paper.Li utilities.

But you could be a bit smarter about it. Suppose you created a list in a utility like Tweetdeck of hand selected people who you know are likely to have something to say that's interesting to your audience. I created one for the intelligent garden which includes the main organic magazines plus the usual suspects from Gardener's World, Joe, Toby, Alys and the rest.

Then I used their widget to embed it into www.intelligentgarden.com site so that whenever anyone goes on there's today's newspaper of relevant stuff.

In situ it looks like this

This has proved to be a powerful tool in spreading the influence of www.theintelligentgarden.com.

Action

OK we're on the last lap – what are you actually going to do? And what results do you want

	Face to Face	Written	Advertising	Social Media & Viral
What do you want to achieve in this area?				
What tangible results do you expect?				
How much will it cost you?				
How will you know you've been successful?				
What 3 things are you going to do differently?				
First approach				
Second Approach				
Third Approach				

Now think about what budget you have, how much time you can spend and how these will support your activities. Most businesses spend 3 or 4% of their revenue on marketing – if you count the cost of selling, total costs are probably nearer 30%

	Hours per week	Money per year
Personal Activity		
Face to Face networking		
Direct Selling		
Exhibitions		
Workshops and Seminars		
Telesales		
Written Materials		
Direct Mail		
PR		
Postcards		
Leaflets		
Email		
Ezines		

Online		
Web Site		
Delivery of Materials via the site		
Google ad-words		
Other online advertising		
Blog		
Linked-in		
Ecademy		
Twitter		
Facebook		

Draw a picture of how you see your marketing activities working together

And last but not least - Who are your top 50 people? You should leave plenty blank at the end for chance encounters and introductions. Good Luck.

Name	Organisation	Relationship	How will you meet them?

Conclusion

You should now have enough information to start developing your marketing promotion plan.

You can decide how much time to spend on line and how to integrate it into an overall vision that will support all your face to face networking and selling activity.

We're assuming here that you have a decent product set aimed at a market place that wants it and that your pricing structure is correct. Getting this offer right is a key part of marketing which we have not addressed in this book. If you need help with researching the market and formulating new products and offers to meet your existing and potential new clients we have spent most of our working lives researching markets and creating and launching new products – so maybe we can help you.

However assuming you have that part sorted, if you've followed the method in the book, by now you should have constructed a story that connects you emotionally with your clients and established what media you want to use to promote it.

Remember – you are trying to generate a flow of leads that you can manage to turn into business – either on the site or later – according to the sales targets that you calculated earlier.

All you need to do is execute it vigorously within the 12 hours a week that you have at your disposal

What else we can do for you

We offer various marketing workshops, courses and services to help you build your presence. The most important are.

1Man Brand – distance learning course on how to market yourself effectively. More details at www.1ManBrand.co.uk

Punch Above your weight – Full day workshop going into the "how to do it" of on line marketing. More details at www.punchaboveyourweight.com

We can offer on going support if you want to apply the principles outlined in this book by acting as an interim marketing director. For instance we offer get you started programmes to help you set up and run Adwords campaigns, start blogging and develop a social network strategy to pull all of your internet presences into a complete, unified programme.

We also offer strategic planning to help you develop and implement a marketing strategy that's aligned to the current and future growth needs of your business.

Finally we can deliver Market Research Services to help you assess your opportunities and find not only the gap in the market but the market in the gap.

Full details of what we do and information on our Track Record can be found at www.howtodobusiness.com.

Or of course you can ring me, Alan Rae on 0845 094 0407 or email at alan@howtodobusiness.com or alan.rae@aiconsultants.co.uk

I wish you luck with your marketing and hope we may be able to help you again in the future.

All the best

Notes

Notes

About Alan Rae

Nowadays I run a family business in Sussex which majors on online sales of plants like lemon and orange trees, herbs and orchids. We also sell Biological Controls and gardening equipment on line and we grow and sell organic vegetables in the real world as Fletching Glasshouses.

I also carry out research projects into how small companies use technology especially the internet to promote themselves and work more effectively and often turn what I find into training materials. Clients over the years include HP, PC World, Business Link, Virgin Atlantic and various UK government agencies like the DTI, SEEDA etc.

Previously I've been a research biochemist (D Phil in plant science) marketing manager of a heavy engineering company, Managing Director of 2 Computer companies and project director of an IT and e-business training centre.

Personal interests include gardening, the environment, windsurfing and playing music.

My current project is www.theintelligentgarden.com which seeks to combine science with organic principles to provide things that intelligent gardeners need and which acts as a practical example of the principles of "Punch Above Your Weight" a training programme for small businesses wanting to learn how to promote themselves online.

This book is in fact the current incarnation of the Punch Above Your Weight Workshop - more details at www.punchaboveyourweight.com

Stuff worth reading

[i] Geoffrey Moore – Inside the Tornado – Capstone – 1995, 1998

[ii] Dudley Lynch – Strategy of the Dolphin

[iii] Grant Leboff – Sales Therapy - Capstone - 2007

[iv] Closing the Gap 3 – Cranfield Institute 2002.

[v] See Albert-Lazlo Barabasi – Linked – Perseus books 2002

[vi] See Albert-lazlo Barabasi – Linked – Perseus books 2002

[vii] Malcolm Gladwell – The Tipping Point- Abacus 2000

[viii] Seth Godin – Unleashing the Idea Virus – Simon and Schuster 2000

[ix] Robert Cialdini – Influence, Science and Practice – Allyn and Bacon 2001

[x] The term Giver's Gain in the list was originated by Dr Ivan Misner, founder of BNI. His ideas are set out in the 29% solution Greenleaf books 2008.

[xi] http://weblogs.hitwise.com/robin-goad/social_networks/

[xii] Robin Dunbar – The Human Story - Faber and Faber 2005

[xiii] Nicholas Christakis and James Fowler – Connected – Harper Collins 2010

[xiv] Penny Power – Know me, Like me , Follow me

[xv] Lisa Harris and Alan Rae – The revenge of the gifted amateur. Journal of Small Business and Enterprise development vol16 no4 2009.

[xvi] I Ching - Richard Wilhelm Translation – Routledge Kegan Paul

[xvii] Robert Cialdini – Influence, Science and Practice – Allyn and Bacon 2001

[xviii] Barry Schwarz – Paradox of Choice – Harper Collins 2005

Lightning Source UK Ltd.
Milton Keynes UK

176951UK00002B/101/P